BÜRO
DESTF

slanted

Büro Destruct 4
by Büro Destruct

Dedicated to Heinz "Heiwid" Widmer.
Our friend and partner who passed away
on the 1st of June 2012.

Slanted Publishers UG
(haftungsbeschränkt)
Nebeniusstrasse 10, 76137 Karlsruhe, Germany
T +49 (0) 721 85148268
info@slanted.de
slanted.de
@slanted_publishers

© Slanted Publishers, Karlsruhe, 2021
Nebeniusstraße 10, 76137 Karlsruhe, Germany

© Design by Büro Destruct
Wasserwerkgasse 7, CH-3011 Bern, Switzerland
bd@burodestruct.net
burodestruct.net
@burodestruct

ISBN: 978-3-948440-27-5
1st edition 2021

Concept & Design: Büro Destruct
Cover: Internship collaboration with Rotjana Linz
Preface: Jens Müller
English translation: Kevin Mueller
Japanese translation: Kazue Schmitt
Publishing Direction: Lars Harmsen, Julia Kahl
Proofreading: Julia Kahl, Bettina Kuntz, Kevin Mueller
Typeface cover: BD Barbeaux
Typeface content: Akzidenz Grotesk
Printing: Stober Medien, stober.de
Paper: Magno Volume, 150 gsm
Cardboard: Algro Design Duo, 380 gsm

The rights of the illustrations, photos,
characters, logotypes and fonts
on pages 66, 67, 120, 121, 214, 215, 226
belong to their respective owners

The German National Library lists this publication in the German
National Bibliography; detailed bibliographic data is available
on the Internet at dnb.d-nb.de

Slanted Publishers is an internationally active independent publishing and media house, founded in 2014 by Lars Harmsen
and Julia Kahl. They publish the award-winning print magazine Slanted, which twice a year focuses on international design
and culture. The Slanted blog www.slanted.de and social media have been publishing daily news and events from the
international design scene and presenting inspiring portfolios from around the world for 17 years. In addition to the Slanted
blog and magazine, Slanted Publishers initiates and creates projects such as the Yearbook of Type, tear-off calendars
Typodarium and Photodarium, independent type foundry VolcanoType and others. Slanted's publishing program reflects their
own diverse interests, focusing on contemporary design and culture, working closely with editors and authors to produce
outstanding publications with meaningful content and high quality. These publications can be found in the Slanted Shop
alongside other extraordinary products by young design talents and established producers from all over the world. Slanted
was born from great passion and has made a name for itself across the globe. Its design is vibrant and inspiring – its philosophy open-minded, tolerant, and curious.

büro

BD:3

Vorwort von Jens Müller

Neben seiner Arbeit als Gestalter forscht Jens Müller über die Geschichte des internationalen Grafikdesigns und ist Autor vielbeachteter Fachbücher, darunter «Logo Modernism» oder «The History of Graphic Design».

Er unterrichtet als Lehrbeauftragter an der Hochschule Düsseldorf / Peter Behrens School of Arts, sowie am Fachbereich Design der Fachhochschule Dortmund.

Monografisch

Macht man sich auf die Suche nach den Ursprüngen gedruckter Designmonografie, kann man bis zu den französischen Plakatkünstlern der Belle Époque zurückgehen. Bereits in den Anfangstagen des Grafikdesigns nutzten Toulouse-Lautrec und seine Kollegen Bücher, um Plakate und andere Drucksachen im Anschluss an ihre zweckgebundene Verwendung zu publizieren und zu konservieren. Seither haben sich Designerinnen und Designer aller Generationen dieses Mediums bedient – zur Selbstinszenierung und Selbstvergewisserung des eigenen Tuns oder schlichtweg, um Rückschau auf das entstandene Werk zu halten. So vielfältig die Beweggründe sind, so verschiedenartig sind auch die Erscheinungsformen der Designmonografie – von kiloschweren Coffee-Table-Publikationen bis zu unprätentiös erscheinenden Lehrbüchern zur jeweiligen grafischen Philosophie. Die Idee, ein Buch als «Sicherungskopie» des eigenen Archivs zu nutzen, scheint vielleicht ein wenig aus der Zeit gefallen. Denkt man an die unzähligen nicht mehr lesbaren CD-Roms oder offline gegangenen Websites, ist das gedruckte und in Auflage verbreitete Buch allerdings noch immer die wohl beste Möglichkeit Text und Bild für die Zukunft zugänglich zu machen.

Der Beweggrund für die erste Monografie von Büro Destruct im Jahr 1999, nur fünf Jahre nach ihrer Gründung, war jedoch nicht etwa der Wunsch die eigenen Arbeiten für die vermeintliche Ewigkeit zu erhalten, sondern schlichtweg eine – damals noch per Fax zugestellte – Anfrage des Verlags Die Gestalten. Ein unverhofftes Angebot, das man nicht ablehnen konnte. So trafen sich ein aufstrebender junger Berliner Verlag und ein aufstrebendes junges Berner Designbüro. Die Monografie, die nahezu alle bis dato entworfenen Arbeiten der Designer enthielt, wurde zu einem weltweiten Bestseller. CD-Covers, Websites, Logos, Plakate, Schriften, aber auch Experimente und Verworfenes wurden auf knapp 200 Seiten zu einem aussergewöhnlichen Remix verbunden. Die Schweizer, die sich und ihr Designbüro bis heute als eine Art Band verstehen, legten mit diesem Buch ein gekonnt komponiertes Album vor. Und wie bei erfolgreichen Bands, folgte auf die Veröffentlichung eine Welttournee – im Falle von Büro Destruct waren es internationale Vorträge, Interviews, Ausstellungen und Anfragen namhafter Auftraggeber.

Die damals Ende Zwanzigjährigen wurden zum Gesicht einer neuen Schweizer Grafik. Im Gegensatz zum strengen und mitunter kühlen Swiss Style der 1960er-Jahre steht Büro Destruct bis heute für Design ohne angezogene Handbremse. Scheinbar alles ist möglich. Es darf humorvoll, laut, bunt und zeitgeistig werden. Gleichzeitig sind Minimalismus, Präzision und handwerkliche Exzellenz in allen ihrer Arbeiten präsent. Werte, die die Berner stark mit der japanischen Kultur verbinden, in der sie über die Jahre Inspiration fanden und immer noch finden. Im Gegensatz zu Emil Ruder und anderen Helden des klassischen Schweizer Grafikdesigns, die sich ebenfalls auf Japan bezogen, steht bei ihnen jedoch eher die wilde Seite der japanischen Kultur Pate. Shibuya statt Steingarten. Wobei jeder, der einmal in Japan unterwegs war, ahnt, dass beides doch irgendwie untrennbar miteinander verbunden ist.

Nur vier Jahre nach dem ersten Buch erschien 2003 der zweite Band. Seither wurde das Format der Monografie in gewisser Regelmäßigkeit genutzt, um das eigene Schaffen zu archivieren und zu reflektieren. Über nunmehr vier Bände lässt sich die Entwicklung des Büros und dessen Arbeiten nachvollziehen. Es gibt weltweit nur wenige Designbüros deren Arbeit so lückenlos publiziert ist. Ein Traum für Designforschende. Zumal die Bücher nicht nur ein Best-of der realisierten Projekte präsentieren, sondern auch Zwischenschritte, Verworfenes, Experimente und Inspiration enthalten. Seit dem ersten Buch wird ganz bewusst auf die dreidimensionale Abbildung von veröffentlichten Buchumschlägen oder Plattenhüllen verzichtet. Dank dieser Entscheidung lassen sich die Entwürfe bis ins Detail betrachten. Ganz nebenbei bleibt immer wieder offen, welche der gezeigten Varianten zur Umsetzung gelangte. Manche Doppelseite kommt gar wie ein Arbeitsfenster der Designsoftware daher. Obwohl die Abbildungen nur minimal erläutert sind, erlaubt die Publikation durch dieses Prinzip einen ganz besonders intensiven Blick über die Schulter und offenbart vieles über die Arbeitsweise von Büro Destruct.

Zu den Arbeiten in diesem neuesten Band, der die vergangenen zwölf Jahren umfasst, gehören so unterschiedliche Projekte wie das Erscheinungsbild für ein Theater, das Design von Snowboard-Jacken und ein Piktogramm-System für den größten Mobilitätsclub der Schweiz. Büro Destruct beweist eindrucksvoll, dass Erfolg und internationale Anerkennung im Grafikdesign nicht nur möglich sind, wenn man sich über eine bestimmte Disziplin definiert, für ausgewählte design-affine Auftraggeber arbeitet oder einen bestimmten Stil immer wieder variiert. Echte Bandbreite – im Visuellen und in der Varianz der Projekte – sind erstaunlicherweise noch immer eine Seltenheit in der Designszene. Die Berner haben es über die vergangenen 27 Jahre erfolgreich vermieden sich festzulegen zu lassen oder es sich in einem abgesteckten Bereich gemütlich zu machen. Gleichzeitig gibt es ihn natürlich: diesen ganz speziellen Destruct-Touch. Eine eigenständige Handschrift, für die sich viele Wort finden ließen, die sich jedoch auch nach mehr als zwei Jahrzehnten am allerbesten durch das Betrachten ihres Schaffens vermittelt.

Previously released books

Gymnastics
Limited Edition 400 Ex.
1997, Büro Destruct

Büro Destruct I
ISBN 3-931126-24-2
1999, Gestalten

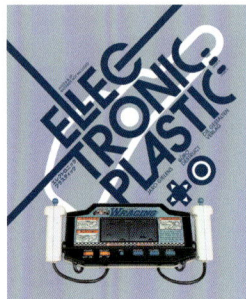

Electronic Plastic
Jaro Gielens
ISBN 3-931126-44-7
2000, Gestalten

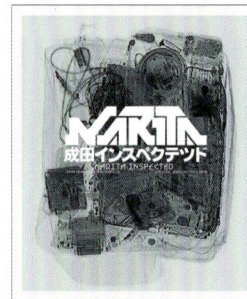

Narita Inspected
ISBN 978-3-931126-61-2
2001, Gestalten

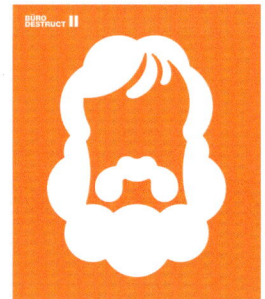

Büro Destruct II
ISBN 3-89955-002-1
2003, Gestalten

Preface by Jens Müller

In addition to his work as a designer, Jens Müller researches the history of international graphic design and is the author of highly regarded reference books, including best-sellers such as "Logo Modernism" and "The History of Graphic Design."

Jens Müller regularly teaches as a lecturer at the Düsseldorf University of Applied Sciences and Arts/Peter Behrens School of Arts and at the Design Department of the Dortmund University of Applied Sciences and Arts.

Monographic

Embarking on a search for the origins of printed design monographs can lead as far back as the French poster artists of the Belle Époque. Even in the early days of graphic design, Toulouse-Lautrec and his colleagues used books to publish and preserve posters and other printed matter once they had served their primary use. Since then, designers of all generations have made use of this medium – for self-reflection and self-assurance of their work or simply to look back on the work they created. As diverse as the motives are, so are the manifestations of the design monograph – from coffee-table publications weighing several kilos to small textbooks on the respective graphic philosophy. The idea of using a book as a "backup copy" of one's archive may seem a bit out of date. However, if one thinks of the countless CD-ROMs that are no longer readable or websites that have gone offline, the published and distributed printed book may still be the best way to make text and image accessible for the future.

The trigger for Büro Destruct's first monograph in 1999 (just five years after the Büro's founding) however was not the desire to preserve their own work for eternity, but simply a faxed request from the publishing house Die Gestalten. An unexpected offer that could not be refused. Thus an up-and-coming young Berlin publishing house and an up-and-coming young design office from Bern met. The monograph, which contained almost all of the designers' work to date, became a worldwide best-seller. CD covers, websites, logos, posters, typefaces, as well as experiments and discarded drafts were combined into an extraordinary remix on almost 200 pages. The Swiss, who to this day see themselves and their design studio as a kind of band, presented a skilfully composed album with this book. And as with successful bands, the release was followed by a world tour – in the case of Büro Destruct, it was international lectures, interviews, exhibitions and inquiries from well-known clients.

Then in their late twenties, they became the face of a new Swiss graphic art. In contrast to the strict and somewhat restrained Swiss Style of the 1960s, Büro Destruct still stands for design without the handbrake on. Apparently everything is possible. It can be humorous, loud, colourful and zeitgeisty. At the same time, minimalism, precision and craftsmanship are present in all their work. The Bernese strongly associate with values inherent in Japanese culture, in which they have found – and continue to find – inspiration over the years. However, unlike Emil Ruder and other heroes of classic Swiss graphic design, who also drew on Japan, they are more inspired by the wild side of Japanese culture. Shibuya instead of a rock garden.

That said, anyone who has ever been to Japan will have realized, that the two are somehow inseparable.

Only four years after the first book, the second volume appeared in 2003. Since then, the monograph format has been used with some regularity to archive and reflect on the artists own work. Over four volumes now, the development of the office and its work can be traced. There are only few design studios in the world whose work has been published so comprehensively. A dream come true for design researchers. Especially since the books not only present the best of the realized projects, but also contain intermediate steps, discards, experiments and inspiration. Since the first book, the three-dimensional illustration of published book covers or record sleeves has been deliberately avoided. Thanks to this decision, the designs can be viewed in detail. It remains unspecified, which of the variants shown was realized. Some double-page spreads even look like a work-space of the design software. Although the illustrations are only minimally explained, this principle allows for a particularly intensive look over the shoulder and reveals much about the working methods of Büro Destruct.

The work in this latest volume, which spans the past twelve years, includes projects as diverse as the corporate identity for a theater, the design of snowboard jackets, and a pictogram system for Switzerland's largest mobility club. Büro Destruct impressively prove that success and international recognition in graphic design are not only possible by defining oneself through a certain discipline, working for selected design-savvy clients or adapting a certain style over and over again. True breadth – in visuals and in the variance of projects – is surprisingly still a rarity in the design scene. Over the past 27 years, the Bernese have successfully avoided being pinned down or getting too comfortable in a defined area. At the same time, of course, it is there: that very special Destruct signature style. An independent handwriting, for which many words could be found, but even after more than two decades it is best conveyed by looking at their work.

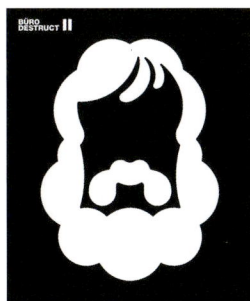

Büro Destruct II Black
Limited Edition 100 Ex.
ISBN 3-89955-002-1
2003, Gestalten

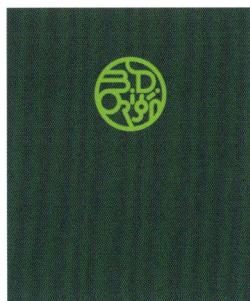

Büro Destruct Origin
Limited Edition 600 Ex.
2004, Gallery Lucy Mackintosh

Büro Destruct III
ISBN 978-3-89955-260-7
2009, Gestalten

Kinder Fragebuch
Krogerus / Tschäppeler
ISBN 978-3-0369-5661-9
2012, Kein & Aber

Büro Destruct Tribler
Limited Edition 650 Ex.
ISBN 978-3-033-04711-2
2014, Büro Destruct

イェンズ・ミュラー氏略歴

デザイナーとしての仕事の傍ら、国際的なグラフィック・デザインの歴史を研究。専門書も手掛け、とりわけ「Logo Modernism」や「The History of Graphic Design」で高い評価を得る。

同氏はドイツのデュッセルドルフ応用科学大学／ペーター・ベーレンス芸術学校、並びにドルトムント応用科学芸術大学のデザイン学科で講師を務める。

モノグラフィック

書籍として刊行されたモノグラフ（デザイン集）の起源を探ると、19世紀末のベル・エポックに華やかなポスターをデザインしたフランスの芸術家にまで遡る。グラフィック・デザインの夜明けとなったこの時代、トゥールーズ＝ロートレックらは書籍を活用して（商品や催し物を紹介するという）ポスター本来の目的を果たしながら、同時にそのデザインを後世に残してきた。以来、この媒体はあらゆる世代のデザイナーに利用されるようになった。自己を演出し、己の行動を確認し、或いは単に自分の生み出した作品を振り返る手段として。デザイナーのこういった多彩な動機を反映するかのように、モノグラフもまた、それぞれの芸術哲学に応じ―コーヒーテーブルの上に平積みされるような分厚く重たい本から飾り気のない教科書まで― 様々な形態を取っていった。自分の作品の「バックアップコピー」として本を利用するという発想は、少し時代遅れかもしれない。だが読み込めめなくなった無数のCD-ROMや、無効になりアクセスできなくなったウェブサイトのことを思えば、印刷され出版された本が、今もなお未来にテキストや画像を残すための最良のメディアなのかもしれない。

設立からわずか5年後の1999年、Büro Destruct（ビュロ・デストラクト）がモノグラフの第1巻出版に至ったきっかけは、作品を永遠に残したいという願望ではなく、出版社 Die Gestalten から（当時はまだファックスで）依頼が舞い込んだためだった。この予期せぬオファーおかげで、独・ベルリンの新進気鋭の出版社と、スイス・ベルンの将来有望な若手デザイン事務所のコラボが成立。それまでに創造されたほぼ全作品を収めた集大成は、世界的なベストセラーとなった。CDカバーやウェブサイト、ロゴ、ポスター、フォント、そして試作品や失敗作に至る全ての作品は、約200頁の奇抜なリミックスとして生まれ変わった。現在も自分たちとデザイン事務所をある種の「バンド」として捉えるビュロ・デストラクトのデザイナーは、この一冊で卓越した構成の「アルバム」を打ち出したのだ。そして成功したバンドと同じく、リリース後にはワールドツアーが続いた。ビュロ・デストラクトの場合、国際的な講演会やインタビュー、展示会などを展開し、著名なクライアントからの依頼が次々に舞い込むようになっていった。

当時20代後半だった若きデザイナーたちは、一躍してスイス・グラフィック業界の新しい顔となった。1960年代の厳格で冷ややかにさえ感じるスイス・スタイルとは対照的に、ビュロ・デストラクトは設立から今日に至るまで、自由な発想のデザインを追求する。ユーモラスで、派手で、カラフルで、時代の精神を反映するデザイン…可能性は無限大だ。それでいて、作品の至る所にミニマリズムや精密さ、卓越した職人芸が息づいている。ビュロ・デストラクトのデザイナーにとって、これは日本文化と強く結びついた価値観でもある。長年に渡り彼らにインスピレーションを与え、今も与え続けている価値観だ。スイスではエミール・ルーダーや他の著名な古典的グラフィック・デザイナーが日本文化をモチーフにしているが、ビュロ・デストラクトが異なるのは、むしろ日本文化の「自由奔放な」面からインスピレーションを得ている点だ。例えて言えば、岩石庭園ではなく、渋谷。もちろん、日本に行ったことのある人なら誰でも知っているように、この二つの側面は切っても切れない関係にあるのだが。

第1巻からわずか4年後の2003年、第2巻が出版された。以来ビュロ・デストラクトのモノグラフは、作品を保存記録し考察する目的も兼ね、定期的に刊行されるようになった。最新刊も含む全4巻には、デザイン事務所や作品の推移が丸ごと収められている。作品がこれだけ完全に公開されているデザインスタジオは世界でも数少ないだろう。デザイン研究家にとって、まるで夢のような話だ。採用されたプロジェクトの他にも、製作途中の作品や失敗作、試作品、発想なども含まれているのだから。但しブックカバーやレコードスリーブといった立体的なイラストは、初版から意図的に除外してきた。この決断のおかげで、デザインのより細かい部分まで観察できる構成になっている。ちなみに、掲載されている複数バージョンのうち、どのデザインが最終的に採用されたかは読者には分からない。また見開きページの中には、デザイン制作のモニター画面さながらのレイアウトも見受けられる。個々のイラストには最小限の説明しか加えられていないが、この原則のおかげで読者はデザインに集中できると共に、ビュロ・デストラクトの仕事ぶりが浮き彫りになっている。

過去12年間の作品を収めた今回の最新刊には、パンフレットやポスターといった劇場の刊行物に始まり、スノーボードジャケットのデザインや、スイス最大の自動車連盟用に手掛けたピクトグラムなど、多岐にわたるプロジェクトが並ぶ。グラフィック・デザインで成功し国際的な認知度を得るためには、芸術分野を特化したり、デザイン好きなクライアントのためだけに仕事をしたり、お決まりのスタイルに手を加えたりするだけが唯一の方法ではないと、ビュロ・デストラクトは印象的に証明している。ビジュアル的にも、プロジェクトの多様性という観点からも、デザイン分野における「真の幅広さ」は、今も驚くほど珍しい。しかしビュロ・デストラクトは過去27年の間にわたり、一つの型にはまることも、自分のテリトリーで慢心することもなかった。それでいて、作品からにじみ出るビュロ・デストラクトの個性。その「独自の筆跡」を表現する言葉は尽きないが、20年以上経った今も、彼らのデザインを見つめればそれがひしひしと伝わってくる。

イェンズ・ミュラー

Above:
**Chestnut Tree
Gymnastics**

Right:
**Din Condensed
Gymnastics**

2018

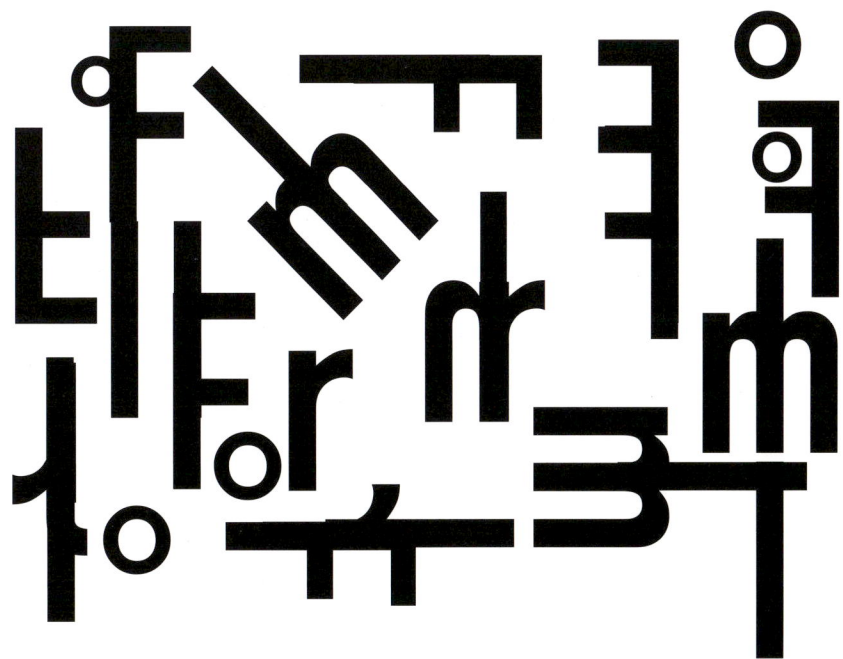

Büro Destruct
Crew portrait photo

From left to right:
Fideljus "HGB" Berger
Heinz "H1" Reber
Marc "MB" Brunner
Lorenz "Lopetz" Gianfreda

Photo: Lieblinge

Winter, 2014

Freibad Weyermannshaus
Bern

**BD intim
and Holy Moments**
Mobilephone pictures
300 × 225 pixel

2009–2021

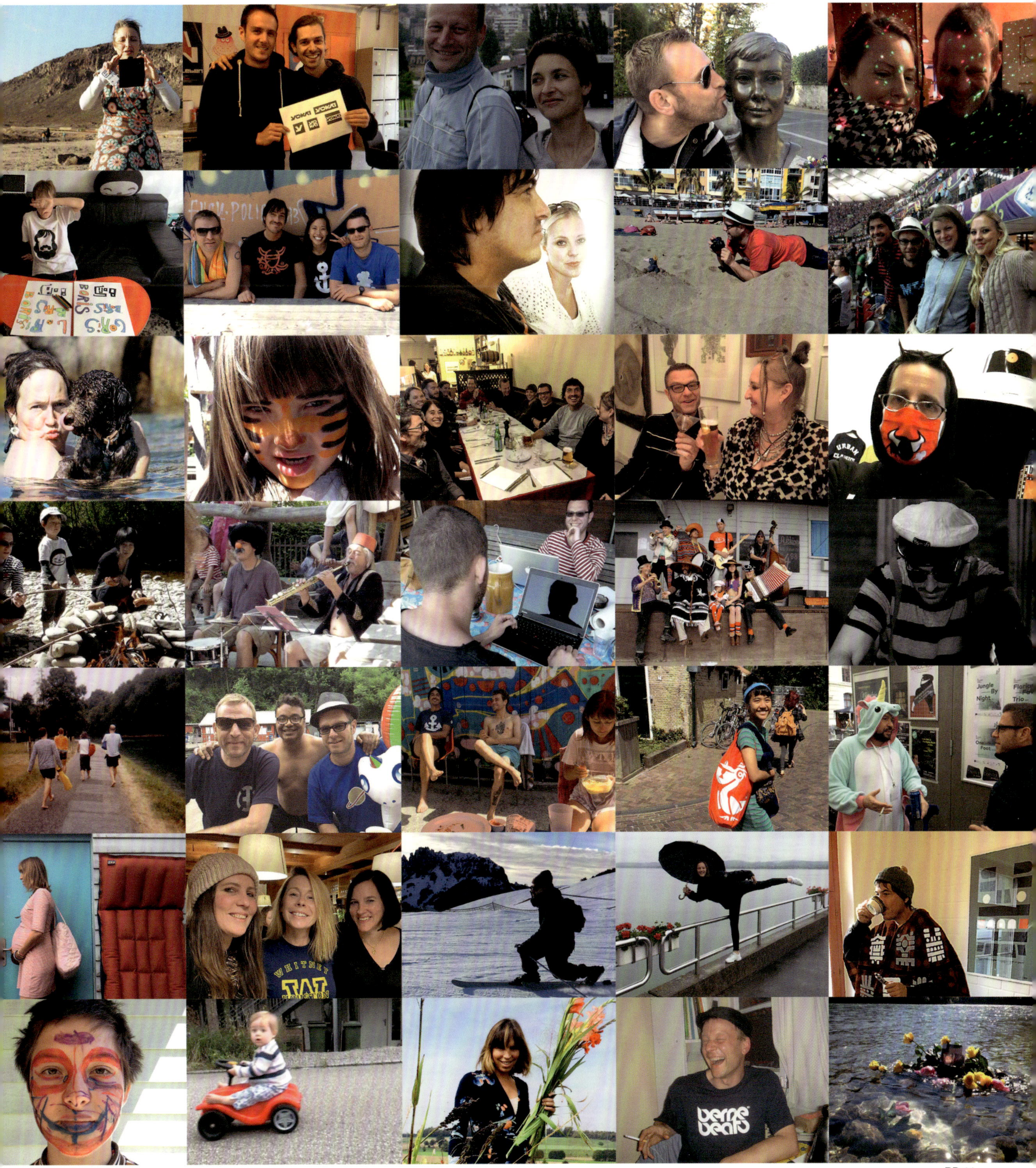
berne beats

Mistery Cow

2020

Strassweid,
Mittelhäusern

Gravity Lander
and "Gravity Lander Pro"
Mobile- and web-game for the
programme "GameCulture"
by Pro Helvetia.
iOS, Android & web.

Programming:
Web & Android: Kaspar Lüthi,
Humantools
iOS: Bataais

Music & Sounds:
Balduin, Creative Cookery

Font "CMOD Subotron"
by Paul Busk

Client:
Schweizerische Kulturstiftung
Pro Helvetia

2011–2012

Discontinued :(

Gravity Lander Pro
App Store game description:

Gravity Lander Pro takes you
on an acrobatic flight into
space.

Help three Cosmonauts on
their mission to master gravity
and debris cluttering the lan-
ding bases on Earth, Moon,
Mars, Jupiter's moon Europa
and Neptune.

Imagine circus acrobatics,
pinball, puzzle action with a
rocket in retro space.
Beware of obstacles like
bumpers, wheels, lifts, ex-
plosives, trampolines and
debris on your flight down to
the safe base. Use boosts
and tilt your device for a new
action experience.

Acrobatic steering skills
and a healthy portion of luck
will help you to succeed the
100 missions.

Features:

Seriously addictive and
intuitive physics gameplay.

100 missions from training,
easy, casual, tricky to hard.

Retro graphics by Swiss
graphic design studio Büro
Destruct.

Cosmic analog synthesizer
soundtrack by Balduin.

Gravity Lander Pro is the
sequel to the successful free
game Gravity Lander.

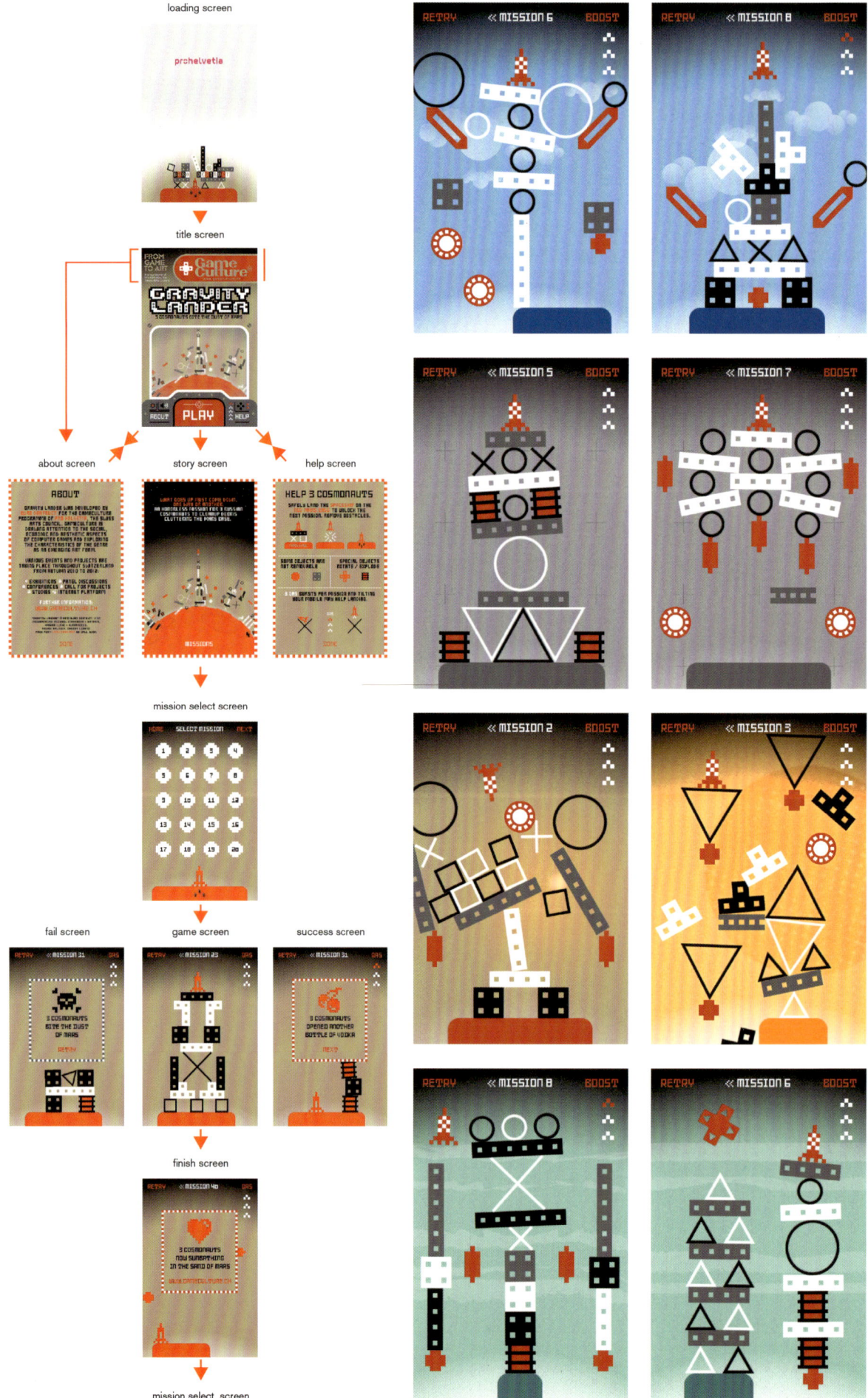

loading screen

title screen

about screen   story screen   help screen

mission select screen

fail screen   game screen   success screen

finish screen

mission select screen

GRAVITY
LANDER

3 COSMONAUTS BITE THE DUST OF MARS

FOUN—DATION AWARD 2020

F+

FÖRDERPREIS FÜR SCHWEIZER JUNGARCHITEKTEN

Foundation Award
Logotype, key-visual
for the ongoing, annual
"Foundation Award" to
support young architects
from Switzerland.

Client:
Computerworks,
Vectorworks

2010

DEETRON

RE←CREATION

RE-CREATION · RE-CREATION

DLPLTD
A / B / C / D

RE) MIXES COMPILED (

CHARACTER® 007

**Deetron – Re-Creation
Remixes Compiled**
DLP sleeve artwork

Client:
Sam Geiser, Deetron

Publlished on Character007

2017

Deetron remixes for Todd Terje,
Ennio Morricone, Osunlade
feat. Divine Essence, Randolph,
Ezel, Huxley and The Juan
Maclean.

BD:17

A BOLD FONT FO EDD

edding 850
permanent marker

TYPEFACE INSIDE!
TYPE-FOR-TYPE.COM

edding e edding

abcdefg a f
hijklmn
pqr n rst
v euv xyz
pqrstuv jn n
xyz z LKN

REDING 85
edding

REDING 850
edding 850

REDING 85
edding 85

REDING
8850

REDING 850

MARKER EDDING NG 850 011-12™

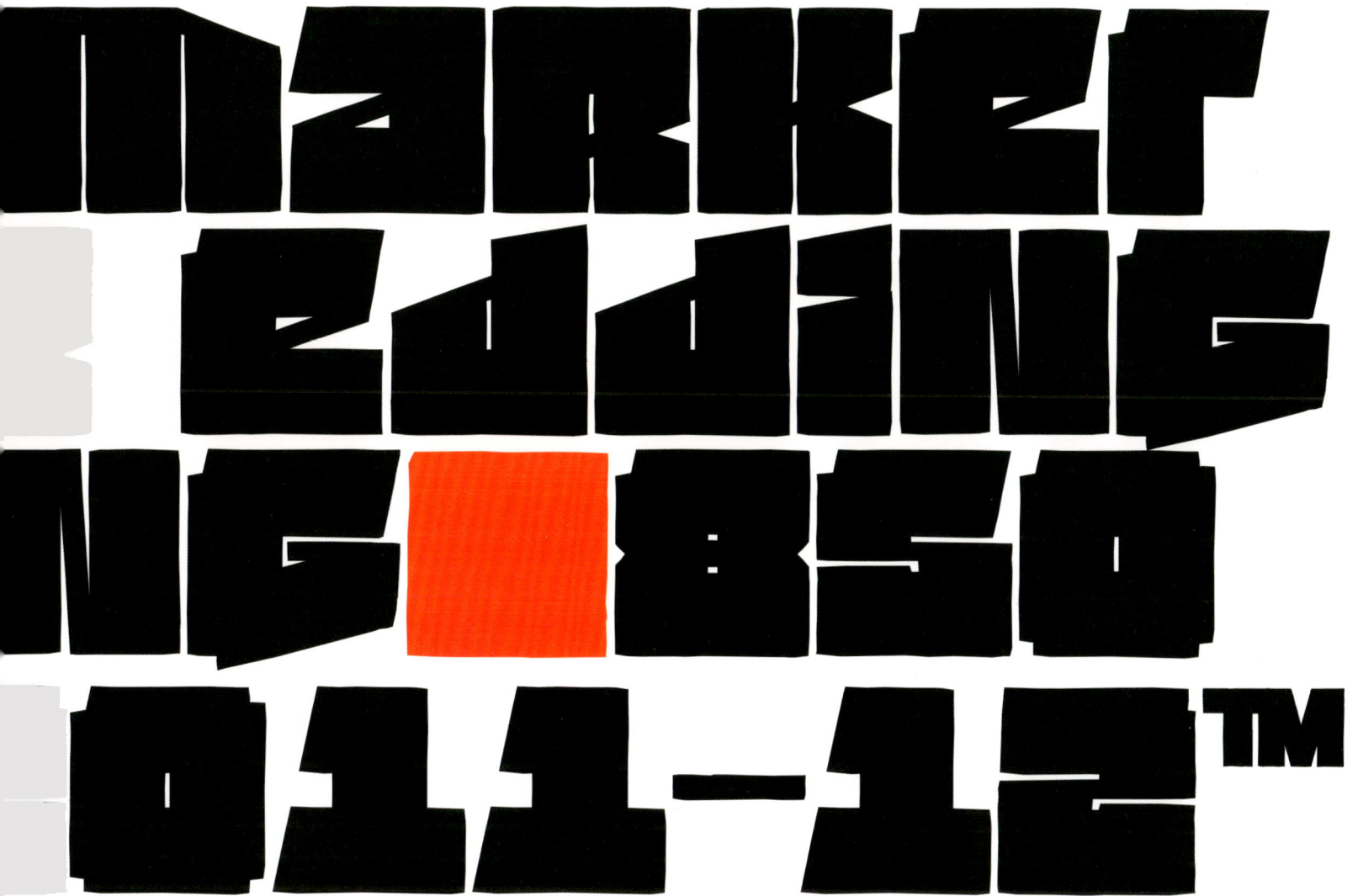

Edding 850 font
Free font to promote the permanent marker Edding 850.

Client:
Kempertrautmann & Shift,
Edding

2011–2012

The font evolved from two simple principles, the thick and the thin stroke, the basics of the marker depending on which way you draw, up/down. Ultimately these two stroke weights create a modular system which can be combined to produce most letters.

Besides the font, the team also built a HTML5 web app which is an endless whiteboard following the principle of edding marker – what has been written, can't be erased.

Our design development of the font was portrayed by director Kai Sehr in a documentary video produced by Snap Film. Animations by OPTIX Digital. Music by Balduin.

Making of video:
vimeo.com/38870492

www.typedifferent.com

ABCDEFGHIJKLMN
OPQRSTUVWXYZ
abcdefghijklmn
opqrstuvwxyz
0123456789
EDDING 850
edding 850
EINGANG

ÀÁÂÃÄÅÆÇÈÉÊËÌ
ÍÎÏÑÒÓÔÕÖ...
...™...[]{}/?...+=×÷-*/
%«»~».""''...„"..._...
...
100% FETT*
„EDDING 850"
«FIRST»

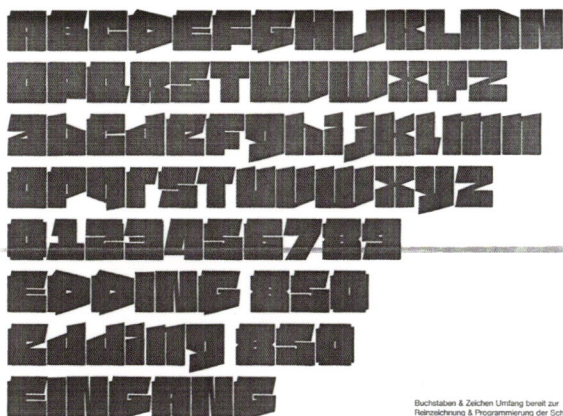

Buchstaben & Zeichen Umfang bereit zur Reinzeichnung & Programmierung der Schrift. Signatur, Agentur:

Buchstaben & Zeichen Umfang bereit zur Reinzeichnung & Programmierung der Schrift. Signatur, Agentur:

DEE TRON FEAT. HERCULES & LOVE AFFAIR CRAVE

DEE TRON FEAT. BEN WESTBEECH RHYTHM

A	A1:	RHYTHM
		ORIGINAL MIX*	[05:54]
	A2:	KAIZORE'S KAYTRONIK DUB REMIX**	[06:10]
B	B1:	WILL SAUL & OCTOBER REMIX***	[06:42]
	B2:	INSTRUMENTAL MIX	[05:53]

WRITTEN BY SAM GEISER, LYRICS BY BEN WESTBEECH, PUBLISHED BY NEWS PUBLISHING & TALPA
* TAKEN FROM THE FORTHCOMING ALBUM "MUSIC OVER MATTER" (MNL P040) ** REMIXED BY KAYTRONIK FOR KOHESIVE / KAYTRONIK PRODUCTIONS @ THE KOHESIVE FACILITY
LAB AND MASTER STUDIOS, MASS RECORDED BY NEIL PICKLES FOR DMACK PRODUCTIONS *** REMIX & ADDITIONAL PRODUCTION BY WILL SAUL & JUSTIN RAYMOND SMITH
DESIGN LOPETZ 2013, BÜRO DESTRUCT BERN CAPITAL

℗ & © 2013 MUSIC MAN / A.K.A & MARKETED AND DISTRIBUTED BY N.E.W.S.
B/MAN. ALL RIGHTS RESERVED. MADE IN BELGIUM.
WWW.DEEJAYBARBONE.DE / WWW.NEWSDISTRIBUTION.NET / WWW.DEETRON.COM

5 414165 061472

DEE TRON FEAT. BEN WESTBEECH RHYTHM

DEE TRON FEAT. OPASOUL OUT OF MY HEAD

OUT OF MY HEAD [7:00]

A	A1:	ORIGINAL MIX
	A2:	GEORGE FITZGERALD REMIX*	[5:01]
B	B1:	KINK VOCAL MIX**	[7:05]
	B2:	KINK DUB**	[7:05]

WRITTEN & PRODUCED BY SAM GEISER, VOCALS AND LYRICS BY OPASOUL/T NEWS PUBLISHING.
* REMIX & ADDITIONAL PRODUCTION BY GEORGE FITZGERALD ** REMIX & ADDITIONAL PRODUCTION BY KINK. DESIGN: LOPETZ 2013, BÜRO DESTRUCT BERN CAPITAL

℗ & © 2013 MUSIC MAN / A.K.A & MARKETED AND DISTRIBUTED BY N.E.W.S.
B/MAN. ALL RIGHTS RESERVED. MADE IN BELGIUM.
WWW.DEEJAYBARBONE.DE / WWW.NEWSDISTRIBUTION.NET / WWW.DEETRON.COM

5 414165 059446

MM 166

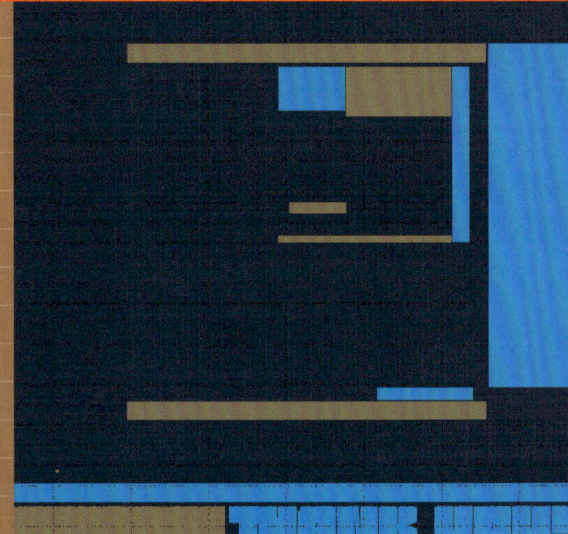

ALL MY LOVE GOES TO SIMONE AND BENJAMIN AND MY EXTENDED FAMILY.
A BIG THANK YOU TO: ALL THE MUSICIANS, REMIXERS AND SINGERS
INVOLVED IN THIS PROJECT; STEFAAN, TOM, KRIS & SANDRA @ MUSIC MAN;
TOON, MARIA & TAIMOUR @ KAZZ; SEBASTIAN THE MASTERING GENIUS;
RIPPERTON THE TECH MASTER & FAMILY; KATE & JACK @ KISH; ALESSIO
IMHOF & FAMILY; LORENZ & LUDOVIC MÜLLER & FAMILY; MORRIS & GLENN
RIESEN & FAMILY, LUIS SANTIAGO ERNI & FAMILY AND SIR WILL SAUL.

DEE TRON MUSIC OVER MATTER

MNL 040

F1	COUNT ON ME*
F2	STRANGE THINGS FEAT. SIMBAD & JUSTIN CHAPMAN
F1	RESCUE FEAT. GEORGE MAPLE***
F2	CAN'T LOVE YOU MORE ****

* WRITTEN BY SAM GEISER ** WRITTEN BY SAM GEISER & SIMBAD, LYRICS BY JUSTIN CHAPMAN *** WRITTEN BY SAM GEISER, LYRICS BY GEORGE MAPLE **** WRITTEN BY SAM GEISER

Left page:
Deetron
12-inch sleeve artworks
"Crave" feat. Hercules & Love
Affair, "Rhythm feat. Ben
Westbeech", "Out of my Head
feat. Ovasoul7"

This page:
"Character EP" label,
"Music Over Matter"
3LP & CD sleeve artwork

2012–2013

Published by News Publishing

Client:
Music Man Records
Gent Belgium,
Sam Geiser, Deetron

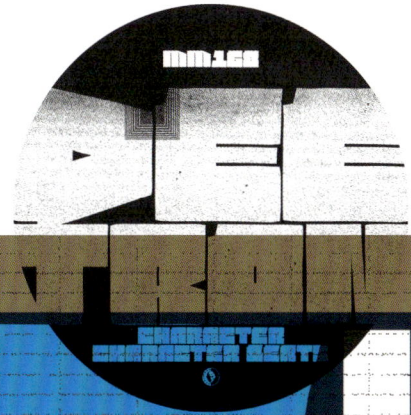

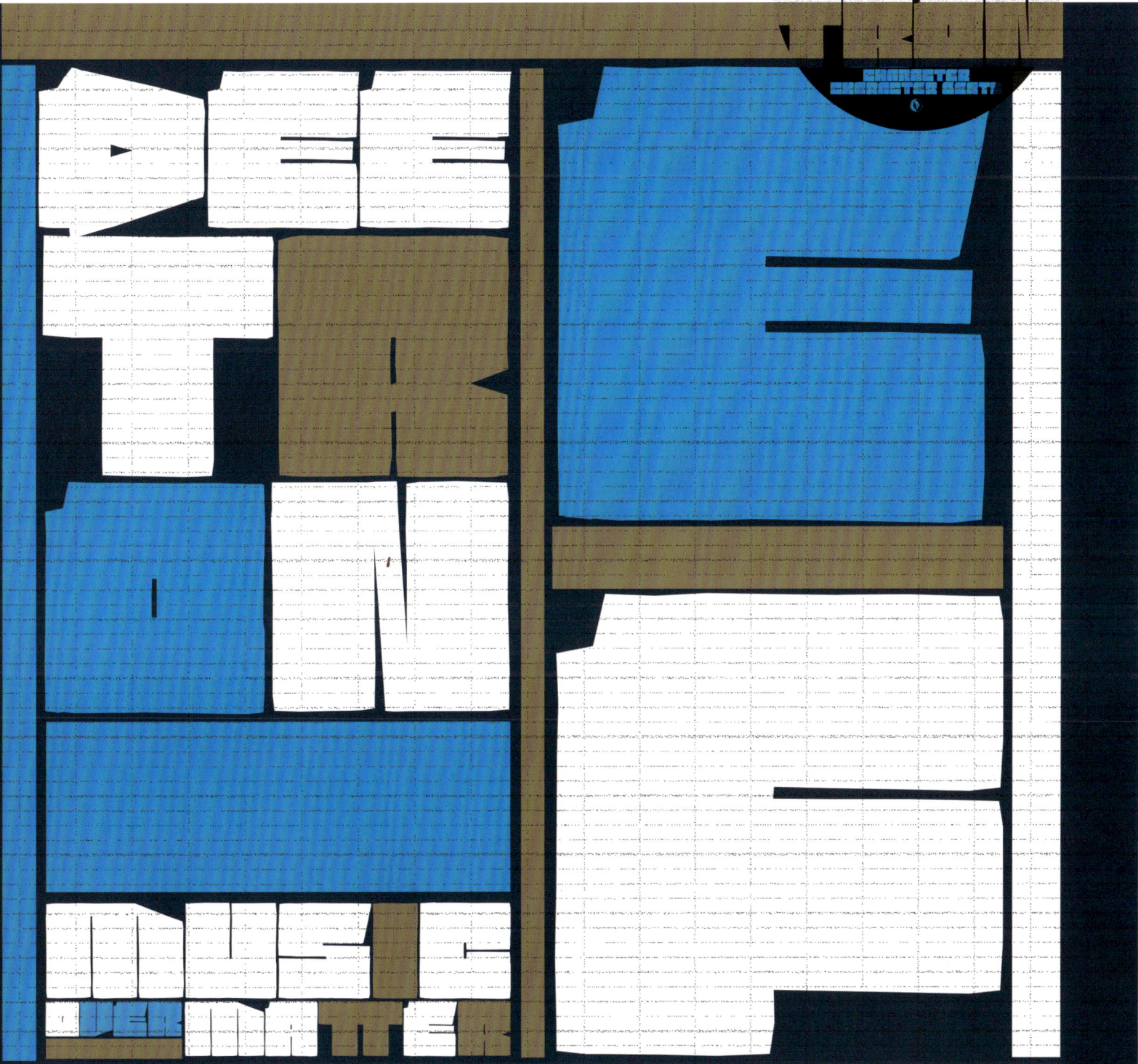

**Alphatronic –
Modulation**
Digital sleeve and download
code-postcard

Published by Everest Records

Client:
Daniel Wihler,
Alphatronic

2020

PROFESS IONELLE DEFORM ATION

Bureau de Struct
professionelle déformation

STRIDE

#9

RÖSSLI BAR

Marcellus

(Unirhythm/Detroit)

Pittman

Thursday
February 20th
2014, Doors 22h
Rössli Bar
Reitschule Bern

lopetz (büro destruct)

STRIDE

#1

Formbar Sandrainstrasse 10 3007 Bern

Sat. January
22nd 2011 Doors 23h

Untold
(Hemlock / Hessle Audio / Hot
flush UK)

Sassy J (Patchwork)
Kev the Head
(Mouthwatering / CUE)

Afterhour by
Princess P (Random
Acoustics)

Sassy J
(Stride, Patchwork)
Kev the Head #13
(Stride)

STRIDE

RON
Morelli
(NYC)

LIES
RECORDS

Thursday December 17th 2015
Doors 21h
Rössli Bar
Reitschule Bern

stridenight.com
RÖSSLI BAR

Played at Stride Night:
Untold
Alex Nut
Lone
Ben Ufo
Al Tourettes
Kowton
Moire
Will Bankhead
Anthony Naples
Madteo
Marcellus Pittman
Greg Beato
Pender Street Steppers
Even Tuell
Ron Morelli
Huerco S
Mother
Kassem Mosse
Rezzett
Sassy J
Kev the Head

Thursday March 10th 2016
Doors 23h
Rössli Bar
Reitschule Bern

Huerco S
(Proibito / Software Recordings, NYC)

stridenight.com
RÖSSLI BAR

STRIDE

#14

Sassy J
(Stride, Patchwork) Kev the Head
(Stride)

Rössli Reitschul: Bern

#6

STRIDE

Friday.21st
February 2013
Kowton
(Bristol UK, Idle Hands
Keysound/Livity Sound/Pole Fire)

Sassy J (Mouthwatering/Stride, Bern CH)
Kev the Head
(Stride, Bern CH)

RÖSSLI BAR

Doors 23h

#12 STRIDE

Even
Tuell
workshop

Sassy J
(Stride, Patchwork)
Kev the Head
(Stride)

stridenight.com
Doors 22h
Rössli Bar Reitschule Bern
Thursday September 10th 2015

RÖSSLI BAR
stridenight.com

Stride Night
Logotype sketches

Client:
Kev the Head,
Sassy J

2010

Stride   STRIDENIGHT   STRIDE NIGHT   STRIDENIGHT   STRIDENIGHT

Stride Night
Clubnight flyers
and posters
105 × 148 mm
420 × 594 mm

Client:
Kev the Head,
Sassy J

2010–2016

#8

STRIDE meets THE TRILOGY TAPES

STRIDE

STRIDE

lopetz (büro destruct)

Greg Beato
(Long Island Electrical
Systems L.I.E.S./Apron)

#10

**Thursday
November 6th**
2014, Doors 22h
Rössli Bar
Reitschule Bern

Sassy J
(Stride, Patchwork,
The Trilogy Tapes)

Kev the Head
(Stride)

RÖSSLI BAR

K Mossem
(Omnika, Workshop, TTT, Wolplaw)

**Thursday
September
15th 2016**

Doors 21h
Rössli Bar
Reitschule
Bern

stridenight.com

RÖSSLI BAR

STRIDE #16

Sassy J   Kev the Head
(Stride, Patchwork)   (Stride)

ReZZeTT
(The Trilogy Tapes, UK)
Live!

**Thursday
November
17th 2016**

Sassy J Kev the Head
(Stride, Patchwork)   (Stride)

STRIDE #17
TTT

Doors 22h
Rössli Bar
Reitschule
Bern

stridenight.com

lopetz büro destruct

#11

STRIDE

STRIDE
Pender
Street
Steppers

Moon Hut
Cassettes

& Hashman
Deejay
(Future Times)

alongside
Sassy J
(Stride, Patchwork)

Kev the Head
(Stride)

#11

Thursday March 5th 2015
Doors 22h
Rössli Bar Reitschule Bern

Stride Night
RÖSSLI BAR
stridenight.com

DOLBY

STRIDE

#5

ISC Club Neubrückstrasse 10 3012 Bern

**Friday.17.
February** 2012

ISC

Al Tourettes
(Applepips/If Symptoms
Persist/GlassTable UK) Live

Sassy J (Patchwork/Stride)
Kev the Head
(Stride)

Doors 22h

CHF 10.– until 23h - come early!

Mother
(Rubadub/ Heated Heads, Glasgow)

Doors 21h
Rössli Bar Bern
Reitschule

**Thursday June 2nd
2016** STRIDE
stridenight.com

Sassy J
(Patchwork,
The Trilogy Tapes,
Stride)
Kev the Head
(Stride)

#15

Alpine Family
Winter postcard
105 × 148 mm

2017

Gardener Family
Spring postcard
105 × 148 mm

2021

Beach Family
Summer postcard
105 × 148 mm

2017

Hiker Family
Autumn postcard
105 × 148 mm

2020

BÜRO DESTRUCT
MONSTER LETTERS
A SPOOKY GATHERING OF THE LETTERS FROM A TO Z

BD Monster Letters
Each letter of the alphabet
represents a monster
character. A spooky gathering
of the letters from A to Z.
A playful, dreadful learning
for kids and the young at heart.

2015

Exhibition poster
700 × 1000 mm

Character posters:
420 × 420 mm each

Paintbook:
100 × 100 mm, 28 pages

Sold out

"BD Monster Letters"
Typedifferent font

www.typedifferent.com

"BD Monsters"
iOS iMessage free sticker app

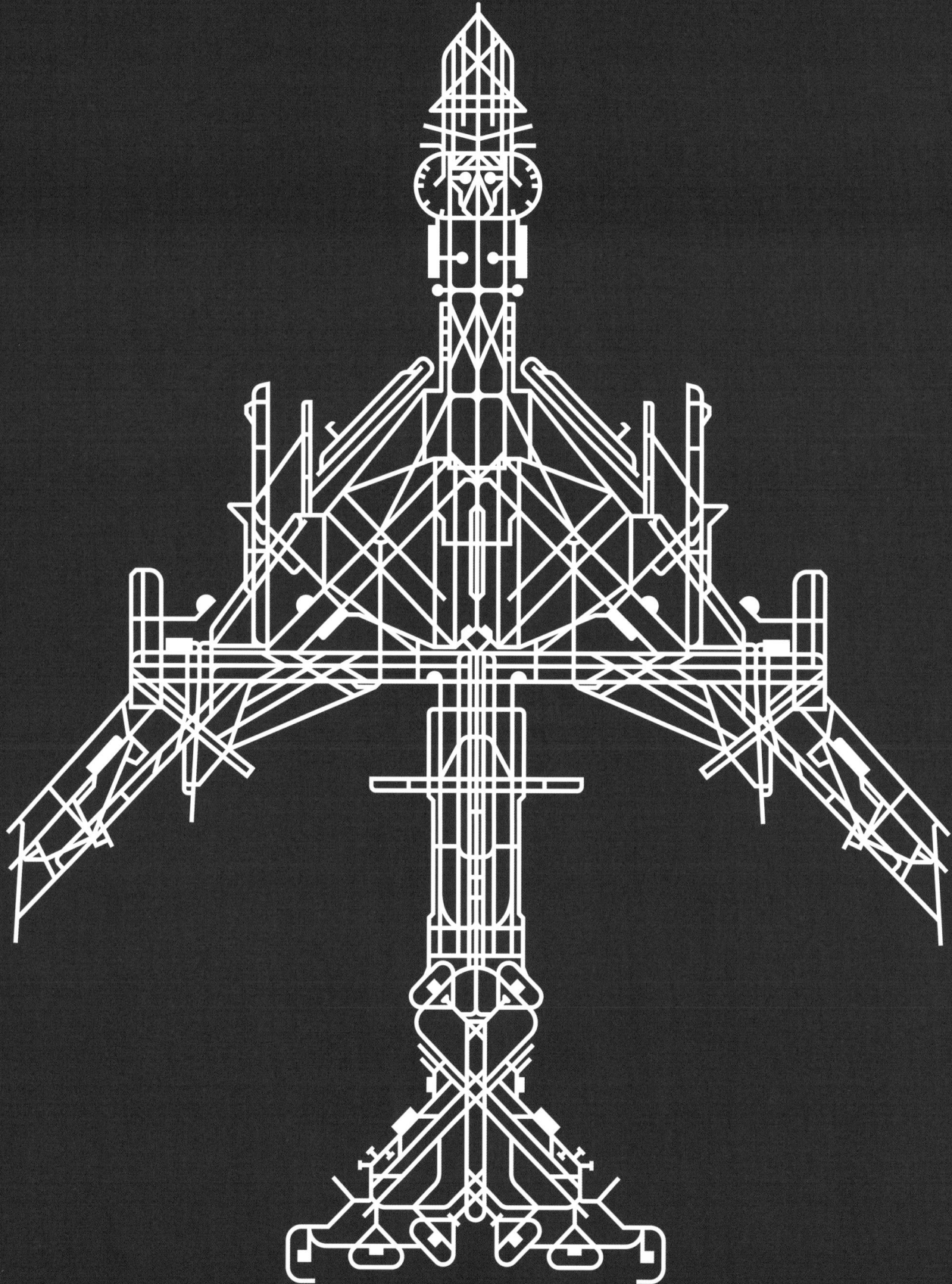

The steepest learning
curves are drawn
in crayon
Poster design for V&A
Museum of Childhood UK.

Client:
AMV BBDO London

2013

Brandt Brauer Frick
Concert poster and flyer
420 × 420 mm
120 × 120 mm

Client:
Reitschule Dachstock, Bern

2016

Right page:
Radio Rabe
20 years anniversary poster
895 × 1280 mm

Client:
Radio Rabe, Bern

2016

!!! EARLY SHOW !!!
MITTWOCH 2. NOVEMBER 2016 AB 19:30
REITSCHULE DACHSTOCK BERN

BRANDT
BRANDT
BRANDT
BRAUER RR
FRICK
FRICK
FRICK

(BECAUSE, THE GYM, !K7, REC / DE)
VVK: STARTICKET.CH & PETZITICKETS.CH

RADIO RABE

95.6 ▪ MHZ

20 JAHRE RaBe

BURODESTRUCT.NET

BD:33

Serigraphie Uldry
Logotype, 50 years
anniversary logotype and
poster designs.
895 × 1280 mm
2685 × 1280 mm

Client:
Serigraphie Uldry

2014–2018

**50 JAHRE
SERIGRAPHIE
ULDRY**

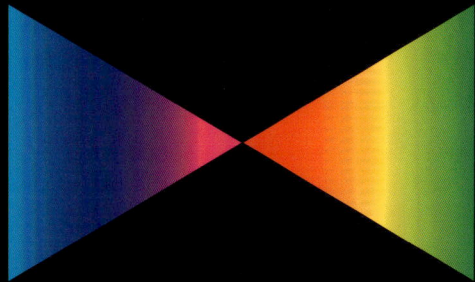

Da Cruz – Eco do Futuro
Logotype, CD sleeve artworks
and visuals.

Published by Boom Jah
Records

Client:
Mariana Da Cruz
& Ane Hebeisen

2017

Bottom:
"Da Cruz"
Logotype sketches

DACRUZ

DACRUZ ✱

DACRUZ

DACRUZ

DaCruz
DaCruz 3

Da
Cruz

Da Cruz

Da Cruz

ECO
DO
FUTURO

ALBUM
OUT
NOW

WWW.DACRUZMUSIC.COM

Summer Blues
Collage and Identity for the
packaging of a beer brewing kit.

Client:
Kitchener, Bern & Sios

2016

Collage sources:
Personal photos from a
restaurant at the Katsura river
in Arashiyama, Kyoto
and vintage Japanese ads.

Right page:
"Blond"
Poster illustration
895 × 1280 mm

Client:
Blond, Salon de Coiffure

Silkprint:
Serigraphie Uldry

2016

SALON DE COIFFURE
MÜNSTERGASSE 22 3011 BERN
031 311 85 15 BLOND.CH

BLOND

UNICORSE

numbers:

#0123456789

lowercase:

ABCDEFGHIJKLMNOPQRSTUVWXYZ

capitals:

ABCDEFGHIJKLMNOPQRSTUVWXYZ

ligatures:

ll ll3ST st ct tt tt ft th ff gg

additionals:

ÂÛÊ Ñ ÕÕ ÃÃ ÄÜ ÄÆ ÏÖÜ ÜÏ ÖÆ É Ñ ÖÜ ÜÆÉ ÖÜÖÔÂ ÂÖÜÂÊ ÖÜÂ ÂŽŠŠ
Þ Þ FZ ƏÐ (! /) ? [] ß ¥ €£ $ % ¢ ¢ □ □ □ □ □ □ Å Æ ¿ ¡
, + ; | + * — ¬ « - » . ‹ ~ › • °' = : \ " . . _ × { ... ‰ } ± ÷)™

BD UNICORSE

0123456789 :

TUNGSTEN MEDIUM

BD WESTWORK

0123456789:

TUNGSTEN MEDIUM

BD KICKROM

0123456789!

FABRIKAT MONO BOLD CAPS

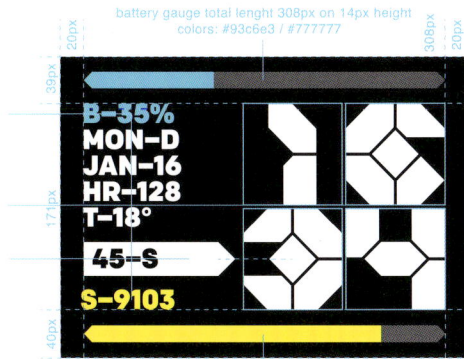

battery gauge total lenght 308px on 14px height
colors: #93c6e3 / #777777

20px 308px 20px
39px 17px 40px

B-35%
MON-D
JAN-16
HR-128
T-18°
45-S
S-9103

steps gauge total lenght 308px on 14px height
colors: #f7f410 / #777777

BD PANZER

1023456789:

COLFAX BOLD CAPS

DT: SUN 9. 7
23:15:04
HR: 89
STPS: 1753

BD Cash-Box

0123456789: .[}

DT: HR: STPS: SUN MON TUE WED THU FRI SAT

Fitbit Watchfaces
Watchface designs for the
Fitbit Ionic & Versa trackers.

2017–2019

The designs are based on the
Büro typedifferent typefaces
"BD Unicorse", "BD Kickrom
Mono", "BD Panzer", "BD
Westwork" and "BD Cashbox".

The watchfaces present all
relevant information at a
glance – such as time, date,
day, battery level, step counter,
heart rate and on some
watchfaces the temperature.

The BD watchfaces are
downloadable for free in the
Fitbit app gallery on iOS and
Android.

Programming:
Mark Reed (Chops)

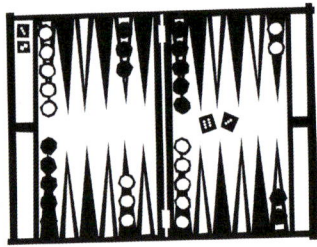

Nerdcore
Illustrations and cover design for a collection of terms related to technology and media explained and written in a short and humorous style by Author Thomas Weibel.

Client:
Thomas Weibel

2015

Illustrations from top left to bottom right:

Backgammon
Pencil
Browser
Computer
Cyborg
Kodak
Larry Laffer
Mastermind
Myst
Natel (Mobile)
Pac Man
Polaroid
Pong
Projector
Radio
Chess
Walkman
Tetris

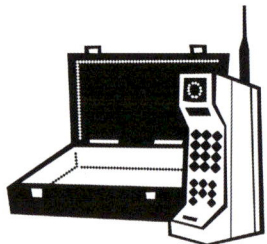

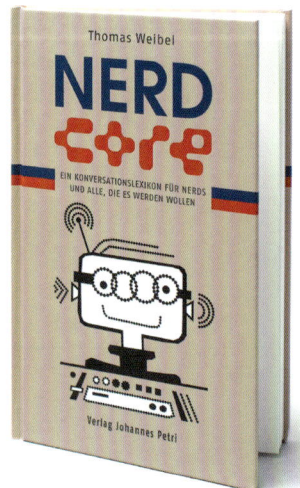

Nerdcore:
Ein Konversationslexikon für Nerds und alle, die es werden wollen

142 pages
193 × 118 mm

Published by:
Verlag Johannes Petri

ISBN 978-3-03784-061-0

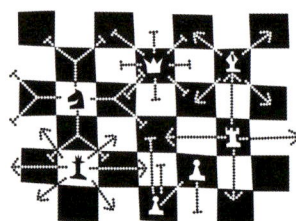

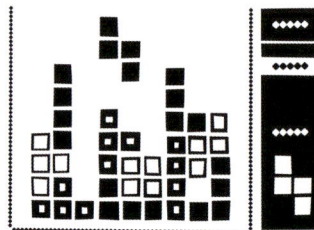

Soft Electronics
Logotype and book cover drafts for Jaro Gielens collection of small household appliances from the 1970s to the 1990s.

Client:
Jaro Gielens

Photos:
Alexander Sucrow

2020

soft
ELECTRONICS

JARO
GIELENS

BÜRO
DESTRUCT

COOKERY
VERLAG

ELECTRONIC PLASTIC FOR THE KITCHEN, BATHROOM & HOME
CONSUMER ELECTRONICS FROM THE 70s TO 90s

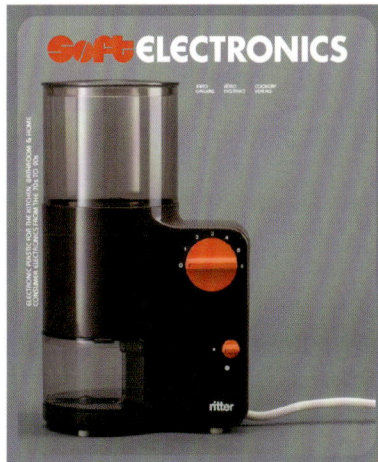

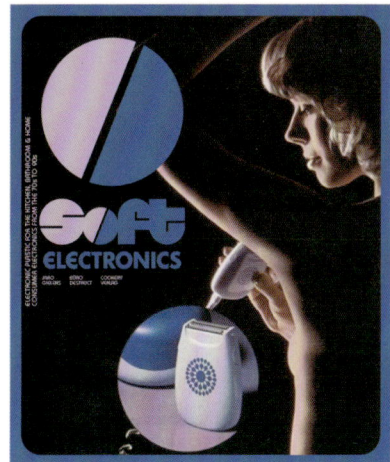

Droppy
Character design

Client:
Jung von Matt/next,
Neoperl, Watersaving.com

2013

Top:
Initial character sketches.

Bottom:
Three favourite vector character
proposals to choose from.

Top:
Selected character mimic
and gesture sketches.

Bottom:
Finalised set of characters
with different mimics
and gestures.

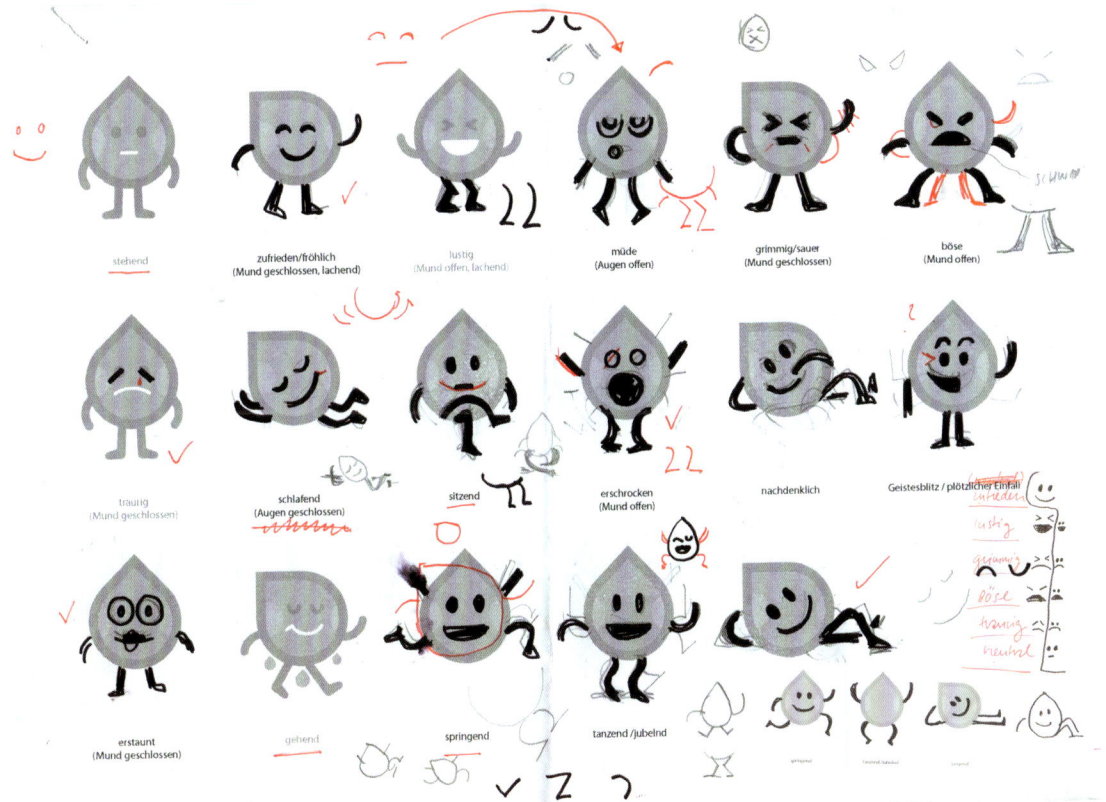

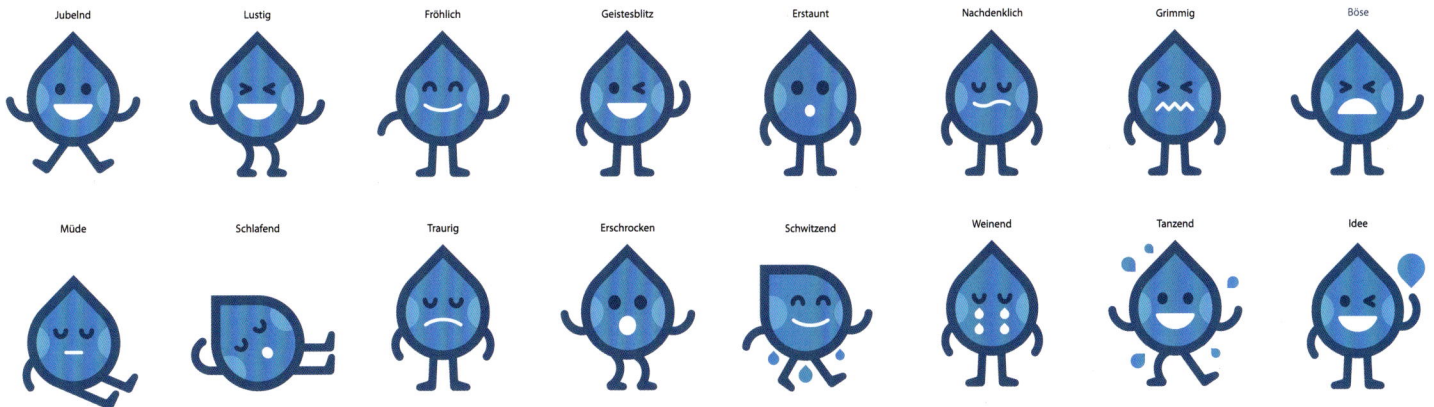

stehend

zufrieden/fröhlich
(Mund geschlossen, lachend)

lustig
(Mund offen, lachend)

müde
(Augen offen)

grimmig/sauer
(Mund geschlossen)

böse
(Mund offen)

traurig
(Mund geschlossen)

schlafend
(Augen geschlossen)

sitzend

erschrocken
(Mund offen)

nachdenklich

Geistesblitz / plötzlicher Einfall

erstaunt
(Mund geschlossen)

gehend

springend

tanzend /jubelnd

WATER
SAVING
.COM

Jubelnd	Lustig	Fröhlich	Geistesblitz	Erstaunt	Nachdenklich	Grimmig	Böse

Müde	Schlafend	Traurig	Erschrocken	Schwitzend	Weinend	Tanzend	Idee

BD:45

The ©opyright

COPY
EDIT
EVOLVE
ENHANCE
PASTE

Bureau de Struct

rogue routinier

Pedaleur
Product pattern designs
for Kitchener.

Client:
Kitchener, Bern

2014

Where do you go?
Poster design for a travel
poster-exhibition at the
bookstore Stauffacher, Bern.
594 × 841 mm

2019

BDR A3MiK

BDR ABMiK
Typedifferent font featuring
Eastern European, Cyrillic
and Katakana characters.

2009

www.typedifferent.com

Icon Kit for Adobe Xd

Adobe has partnered with three world-renowned designers such as Lance Wyman, Anton & Irene and Büro Destruct to create free icon kits consisting of 15 icons each to use in "Adobe Xd".

Client:
Adobe Systems Incorporated
San Jose, CA United States

2018

For our set we gave us some limitations: A maximum dimension of 24 × 24 pixels per icon and just two highly contrasting line thicknesses – one bold (the highway) and one thin (the footpath).

When working on something that should be simple and clean, designers are walking on a tightrope. You may either fall on the side of simple and boring, or you can come up with something simple and surprising. We were looking for a minimalistic, yet radical result.

Right:
Early sketches of the icons

Middle:
The official icon set

Bottom:
Additional icons

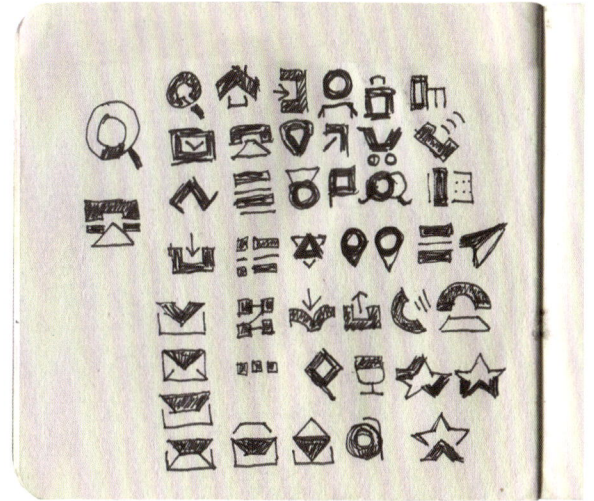

 Search

 Home

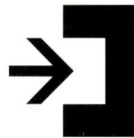 Login

User

 Password

Mail

Telephone

Map Pointer

Send

 Cart

 Walking Route

 Itinerary

 Favorite

Place of Interest

 Chat

   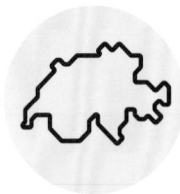   

3 4 5 6 7 8 9

TCS Icons
Extensive set of icons
for print and web.

Client:
TCS, Touring Club
Suisse

2016–2018

BD:53

Right page:
Pepita
Poster design contest
submission dedicating
"100 years Herbert Leupin".
895 × 1280 mm

Client:
Mineralquelle Eptingen AG

2017

Herbert Leupin was a Swiss
graphic designer known
primarily for his poster art.

As an homage in respect
we reimagined how Herbert
Leupin would have designed a
poster for the Swiss grapefruit
soft drink called "Pepita" in
the year 2017.

Left:
First sketches and early drafts

BD:55

Too Late Show
Logotype and illustrations for the promotion of the live late night show called "Too Late Show".

Client:
Das Projektariat,
Till Könneker

Photo: Rob Lewis

2015–2018

For each show the hosts and talkshow guests were sketched by pencils first and then reworked in Adobe Illustrator with a custom made vectorbrush.

LIVE!

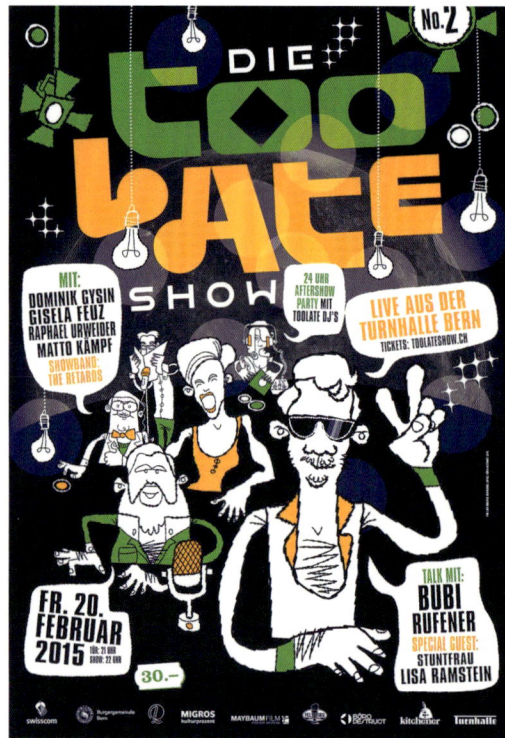

Too Late Show
Posters
420 × 597 mm

Client:
Das Projektariat,
Till Könneker

2015–2018

Hosts:
Dominik Gysin
Gisela Feuz
Raphael Urweider
Matto Kämpf
King Pepe

Showband: The Retards

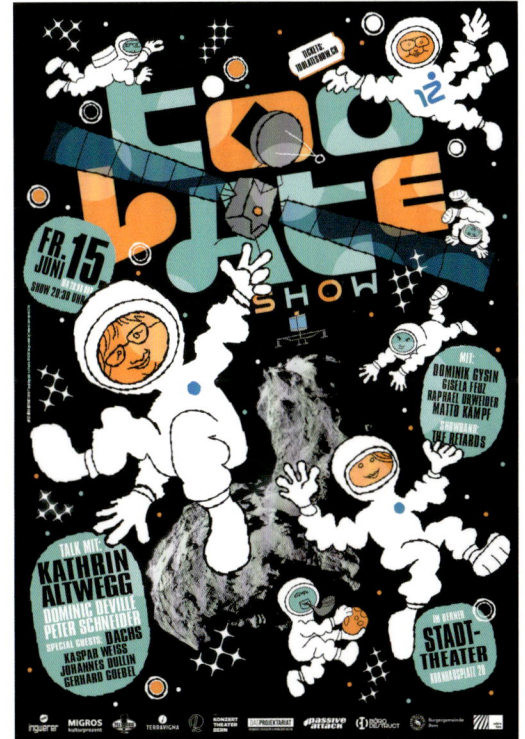

Guests:
Reverend Beat-man
Swiss Wrestling Entertainment
Bubi Rufener
Lisa Ramstein
Adolf Ogi
Play Patrik
Pablo Nouvelle
Christian Kropf
Jennifer Gasser
Kaiser & Dimitri
Müslüm

Güzin Kar
Clausette La Trine
Kurt Aeschbacher
Steff La Cheffe
Aline Trede
Santosh Aertotth
Herr & Frau Schneuwly
Greis
Jonathan Loosli
Kaspar Weiss
Robin Adams
Franz Hohler

Lisa Catena
Raymond Fein
Papst Franziskus
Mario Batkovic
True
Kathrin Altwegg
Dominic Deville
Peter Schneider
Dachs
Johannes Dulin
Gerhard Goebel
Baze

BD

bd retrocentric

RETRO & CENTRIC

123*
456
789
#0

ABCDFGHIJKLMN
OPQRSTUVWXYZ

abcdefghijklmnopqrstuvwxyz
ÂÃÄÆÐÈÉÊÎÍÎŁÑÒÓÔÕŒÙÚÛŮŠÝ
âãäáâãâãæ¢çđèéêëîíñòóôõöðœùúûüuŠßý
#€¥£$&!?.,;:=≈<>^/\|[<>≤≥•*°□«»×[`´˜¨˝¸˛„‚

«Citroën 2CV»
French: Deux Chevaux
Vapeur Was An Economy
Car Produced By The
French Automaker Citroën
From 1949 To 1990

Renault   Peugeot   Citroën

Left page:
BD Retrocentric
Typedifferent font

2009

www.typedifferent.com

Italica
Poster design for the
exhibition "Italian design
is coming home – to
Switzerland".
500×700 mm

2011

Helvetica

Italica

hh h   hhhhh
eeeee eee   el
I IIIIIIIIIIIII lv
vvv   vvvvvv
vv e ee eee   e
e tttttt t tttt t
tttttiiiiiiii iii   i
iiiic cc   cccc c
c aa aa   a a

Helvetica
Typographic pattern design
for a drinking bottle give-away

Client:
Federal Department
of Foreign Affairs FDFA,
Presence Switzerland

2018

hhhh
eee e
IIIIIII lv
vvvvv
e eee
t t tttt
iiiii iii
cccc
a aa

© FDFA Presence Switzerland | Design: Büro Destruct

Switzerland.

Svizra   Schweiz   Switzerland

Svizzera   Suisse

Switzerland
Typographic pattern design
for napkins. The country
name shown in its four native
languages.

Client:
Federal Department
of Foreign Affairs FDFA,
Presence Switzerland

2016

Bärni Bär
Inofficial Bern bear mascot
character design.

Sketches, press articles and
merchandise products.

2010–2020

Bärni Bär

МОЙ МИШКА

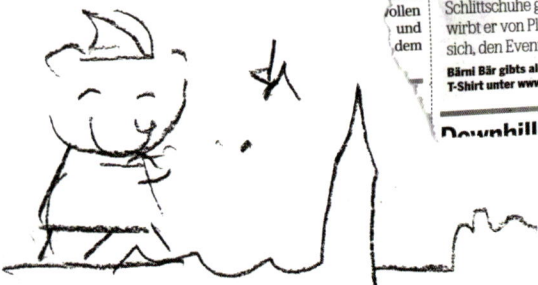

Irohe
Weihnachten

Bärni Bär

Hard2Buff
Logotype for streetwear,
graffiti supplies and urban arts
online shop.

Client:
BD Productions GmbH

2017

www.hard2buff.com

BD

HARD 2 BUFF.COM
BLACK IN STOCK EVERYDAY

HARD 2 BUFF
BLACK IN STOCK EVERYDAY

qualité

BD Barbeaux

BD Barbeaux Numérique

BD Barbeaux

Regular

Cécile se baigne promène danse s'amuse

Amélie Un sujet photographique sur Saint-Tropez

Dorothée Ginsbourg le verbe aimer

Françoise Rouvel qualité la belle de

Lorsque Catherine, encore adolescente, apparut dans les rues de Marseille, plus d'un homme, ému et inspiré par ses formes chaleureuses, se découvrit une vocation de grand peintre. Certains amateurs éclairés de peinture, précisèrent leur pensée en s'exclamant Quel beau Renoir ! » sans se douter que ce nom célèbre allait jouer un rôle décisif dans l'avenir de la jeune fille. Née trop tard pour servir de modèle au sensuel Auguste Renoir, Catherine Rouvel, très tôt, s'intéressa aux chefs-d'œuvre de Jean, metteur en scène et fils du peintre. Un jour, la petite provinciale provençale décida de « monter » à Paris afin de découvrir au Musée du Cinéma certains « Renoir » peu connus. Tandis qu'elle faisait la connais

manteau pèlerine col et petit chapeau

Marguerite par leurs gestes de nonchalance

Joséphine

ビュロ
ロユビ
BÜRO
DESTRUCT
デストラクト

Reine
sans
rênes
Renata

Dans les cabines d'essayage, dans les studios des plus grands photographes de mode, ces halles

BD Barbeaux

ABCDEFGHIJKLMNOPQRSTUVWXYZ
abcdefghijklmnopqrstuvwxyz
0123456789
[\]^_`!"#.ı&'()*+,-./f:;<=>?@°´˜
ÅåÕÖÜüØ¢¢£Ÿ¥€$.ı¿¡""-ß©©
áâàÅéêèë íîìï ſ{}ãõñÑ
óôòÚÛÙæŒ´˜ ø... — ⁶⁹>°ˆ ~

BD Barbeaux Numérique

ABCDEFGHIJKLMNOPQRSTUVWXYZ
abcdefghijklmnopqrstuvwxyz
0123456789
[\]^_`!"#.ı&'()*+,-./f:;<=>?@°´˜
ÅåÕÖÜüØ¢¢£Ÿ¥€$.ı¿¡""-ß©©
áâàÅéêèë íîìï ſ{}ãõñÑ
óôòÚÛÙæŒ´˜ ø... — ⁶⁹>°ˆ ~

BD:67

Typedifferent Font Stencils
The Büro Destruct font
library typedifferent presents
a selection of BD typefaces
as stencils.

340×170 mm

Theses stencils literally liberate
the fonts from their use on
computers.

Produced together with Norrm
and Unkl347 for the Büro
Destruct, "Small City – Big Design" lecture, panel discussion
and exhibition with exclusive
BD products at Bandung,
Indonesia.

2013–2014

Sold Out

Fonts:
Blue: BD Hell (2002)
Green: BD Panzer (2006)
Orange: BDR A3Mik (2009)
Red: BD Doomed (1998)
Yellow: BD Motra (2008)

Typedifferent Stencils
In action at Grafik14
exhibition Zurich.

2014

Right:
**Black Space Race –
A Supersonic Afrobeat
Performance"**
Theater poster
895 × 1280 mm
420 × 594 mm

Client:
Manaka Empowerment
Productions, Schlachthaus
Theater Bern

2018

AFROFUTURE
BY MANAKA EMPOWERMENT PROD.

SCHLACHTHAUS THEATER BERN

«LOOK AT THAT TREE» BECAUSE I CAN SEE THE TREE.
I CAN GO TO THE TREE.
IT'S THE SAME WITH THE MOON.»
EDWARD MUKUKA NKOLOSO
ZAMBIA NATIONAL ACADEMY OF SCIENE
SPACE RESEARCH AND PHILOSOPHY

AFROPETZ 2020: BÜRO DESTRUCT ZAMBIA

BLACK SPACE RACE

A SUPERSONIC AFROBEAT PERFORMANCE

ROBIN ADAMS

WAEL SAMI ELKHOLY

NTANDO CELE

ANGELA KERRISON

DEC·2018
22·PREMIERE
27·
28·
29·
30·
31·& PARTY WITH DJ BAM BIZ-AY

SCHLACHTHAUS
THEATER
BERN

MUSICIANS:
TEVFIK KUYAS / MAZE KÜNZLER /
UELI KEMPTER / KEVIN CHESHAM /
MORY SAMB
MUSIC:
RAPHAEL URWEIDER / MAZE KÜNZLER /
JAMES GRUNTZ / SIMON HO
COPRODUCTION:
SCHLACHTHAUS THEATER, PRAIRIE
TICKETS:
MÜNSTERGASS-BUCHHANDLUNG /
BODAY BULLONI /
WWW.SCHLACHTHAUS.CH

KulturStadtBern   SWISSLOS   ERNST GÖHNER   die Mobiliar   MIGROS   Pro Scientia
                    Kultur Kanton Bern   STIFTUNG   sit 8764

Top left to bottom right:
Zum Glück
Musical poster
297 × 594 mm

2012

Weg
Theater poster
420 × 594 mm

2019

Hotel Kosmos
Theater poster
420 × 594 mm

2015

Frisches Blut
Theater poster
420 × 594 mm

2014

Right page:
25 Jahre Club 111
Frisches Blut, Popeye's
Godda Blues, Ich ohne
aufzufallen, Spaceboard
Galuga. Theater poster.
420 × 594 mm

2014

Client:
Theater Club 111

Schauspielhaus Zürich
Der Besuch
der alten
Dame

von Friedrich Dürrenmatt
Regie Viktor Bodó
Pfauen

Schauspielhaus Zürich
Der neue
Himmel

Uraufführung
Koproduktion mit dem
Deutschen Theater Berlin
von Nolte Decar
Regie: Sebastian Kreyer
Schiffbau/Box

Schauspielhaus Zürich
Nachtstück

Uraufführung
Schiffbau/Box
Projekt ohne Worte
Perkussion Fritz Hauser
Regie Barbara Frey

Schauspielhaus Zürich
Meer

von Jon Fosse
Regie: Barbara Frey
Deutschsprachige Erstaufführung
Pfauen

Schauspielhaus Zürich
Die Jungfrau
von Orleans

von Friedrich Schiller
mit einem Text von Peter Stamm
Regie: Stephan Kimmig
Pfauen

Schauspielhaus Zürich
Hexenjagd

von Arthur Miller
Regie Jan Bosse
Schiffbau/Halle

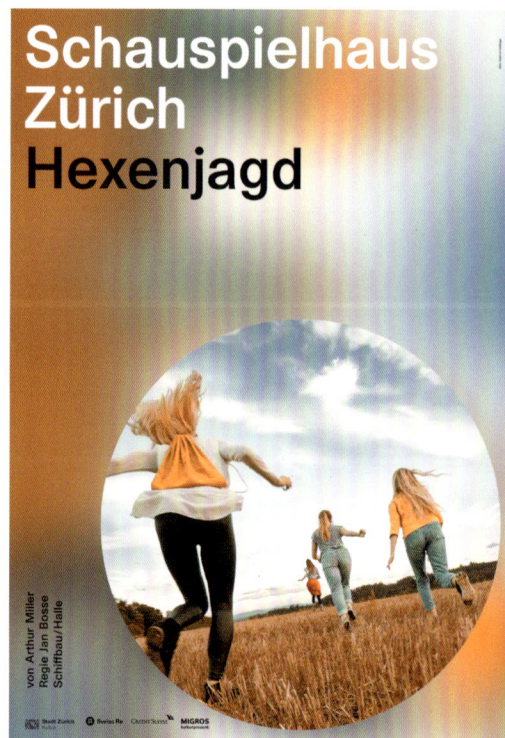

Theater posters
895 × 1280 mm
420 × 210 mm

Photos: Lieblinge

Client:
Schauspielhaus Zürich

2015–2016

Top left to bottom right:
Der Besuch der alten Dame
Der neue Himmel
Nachtstück
Meer
Die Jungfrau von Orleans
Hexenjagd

Right page:
Wer hat Angst vor Hugo Wolf

BD:74

Schauspielhaus Zürich

Wer hat Angst vor Hugo Wolf?

Ein Liederabend von Herbert Fritsch
Regie Herbert Fritsch
Uraufführung
Pfauen

büro destruct

Stadt Zürich Kultur   Swiss Re   CREDIT SUISSE   MIGROS kulturprozent

BD:75

Anglerfish
Character design for "HYT
Watches" drybag give-away.

Client:
HYT Watches

2018

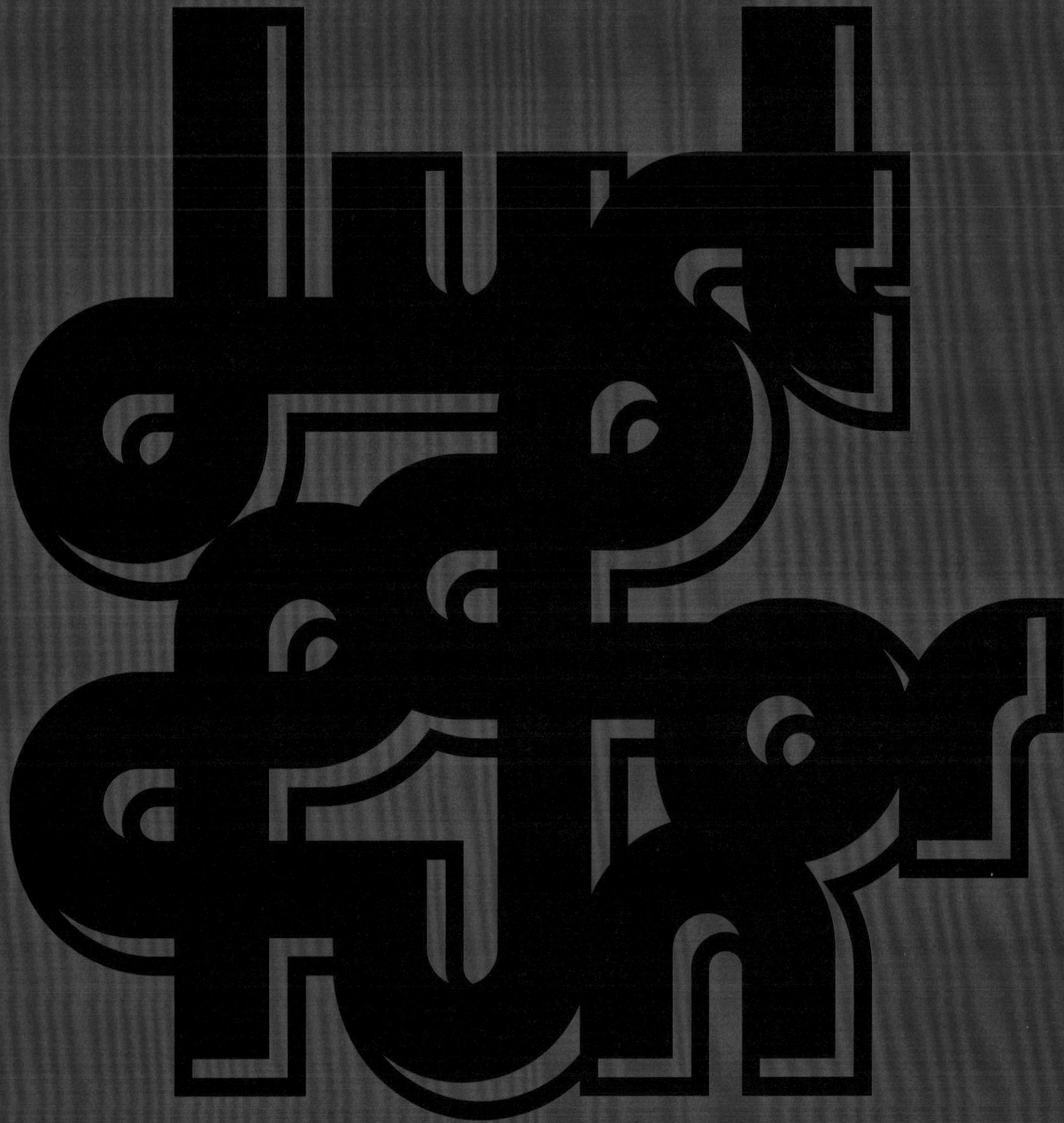

Just defunct

Bureau de Struct

less budget – more freedom

Right page:
SwissGames
Stickersheet
148 × 210 mm

Client:
SwissGames,
Pro Helvetia

2019

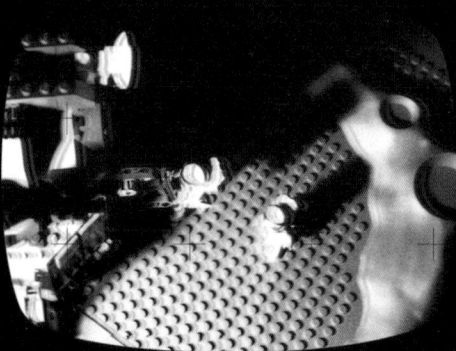 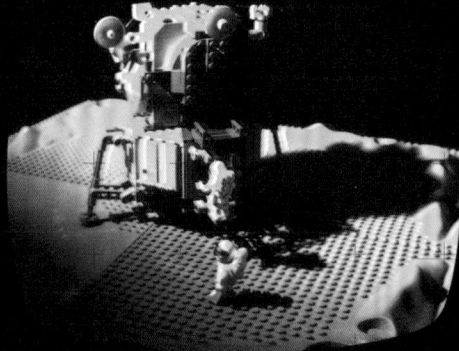 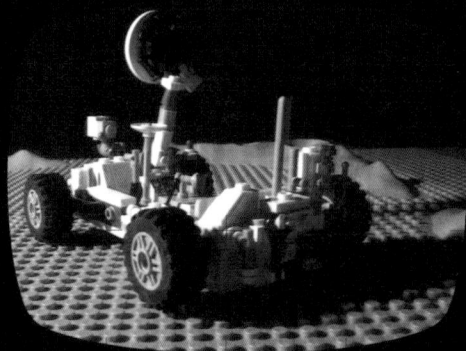

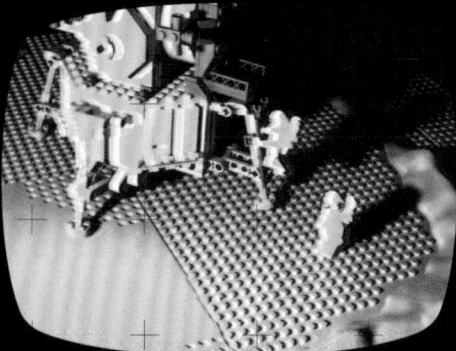  

SWISS GAMES

EXPORTING FUN &
INNOVATION WORLWIDE
initiated by Pro Helvetia
the Swiss Arts Council

SWISSGAMES

MY GAME IS

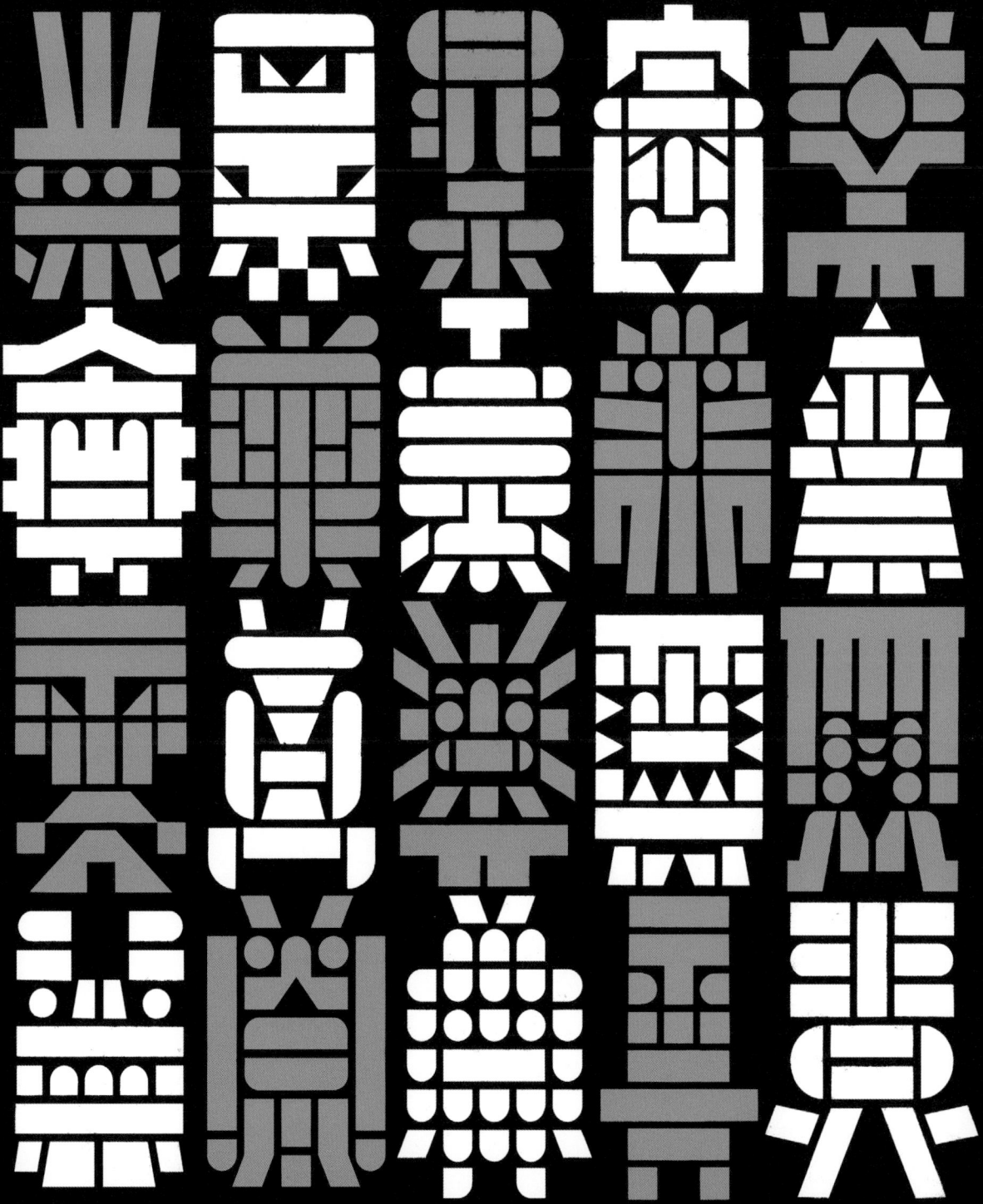

BÜRO
20 YEARS BÜRO DESTRUCT
<20.0
+
SERIGRAPHIE
50 YEARS SERIGRAPHIE ULDRY
50

DESTRUCT ULDRY

ANNIVERSARY
EXHIBITION
TRIBLER

SAMSTAG 1. NOVEMBER 2014
17:00 UHR
SOON GALLERY
LORRAINESTRASSE 69
CH-3013 BERN

SOON

Previous page:
Tribler – 20 years
BD anniversary exhibition
Event poster and flyer
895 × 1280 mm
420 × 210 mm

2014

Silk-screen prints:
Serigraphie Uldry

Right:
Tribler Sun
Original stencil

Bottom:
Sources of inspiration
and 20 years BD logotype

"Kanji" street paint in Japan

Ancient Chinese "I Ching"

20 YEARS
BÜRO
DESTRUCT

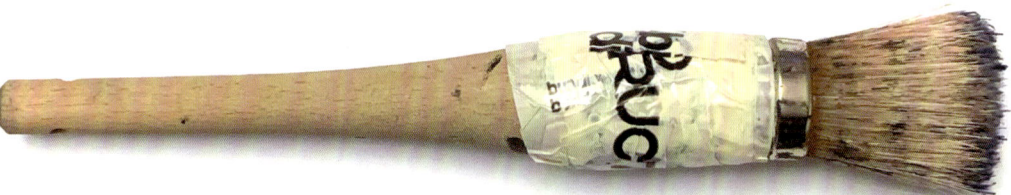

Tribler Book

The Tribler book characterizes, documents and catalogs twenty mythical creatures, idols and demons of the Tribler clan, based on text and image material. With a generous dose of humour, it reflects attitude of Büro Destruct.

In the event of the twentieth anniversary of Büro Destruct, the graphic designers from Bern explore their origins and the things that inspired them over the years. Every single Tribler symbolizes a working year of the graphic design collective. This is particularly apparent in the form of artifacts and sources of inspiration on the respective double page after the presentation of each Tribler character.

With a foreword by Gregor M. Wildermann
Limited edition of 650 copies, hardcover, 96 pages
Languages: English & German
214 × 265 mm

Published by Büro Destruct
ISBN 978-3-033-04711-2

2014

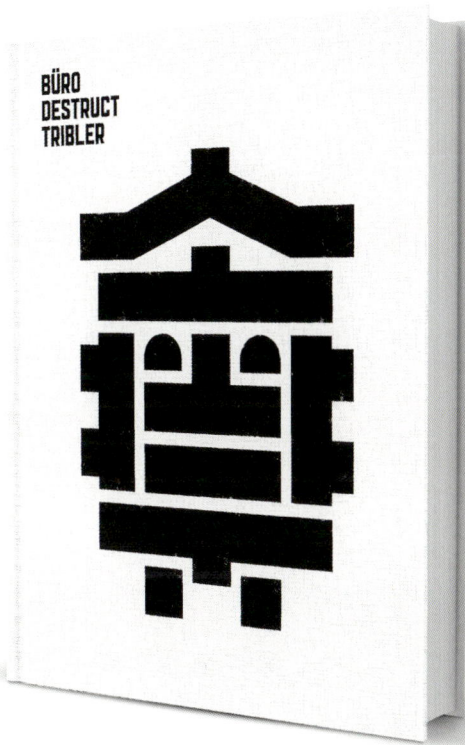

Right:
"Tribler, 20 years
BD anniversary exhibition"
at Soon Gallery.
1st November 2014.

Bottom:
Two spreads from the Tribler book.

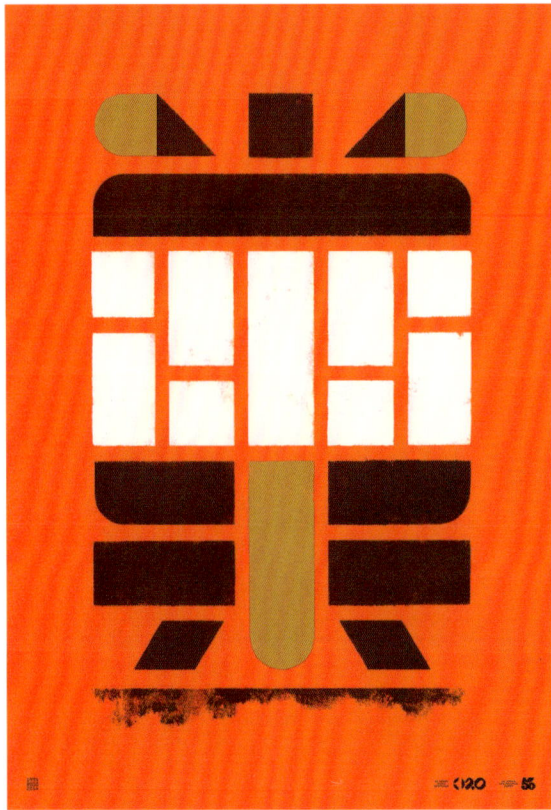

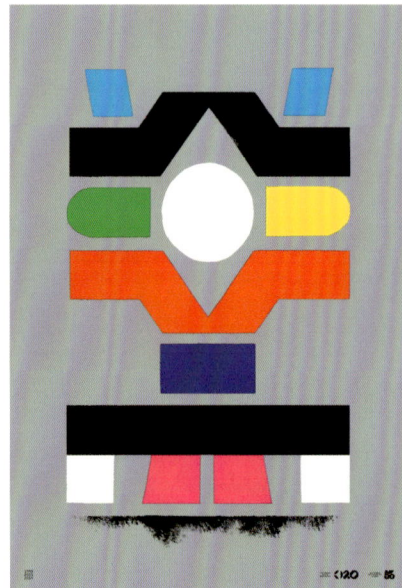

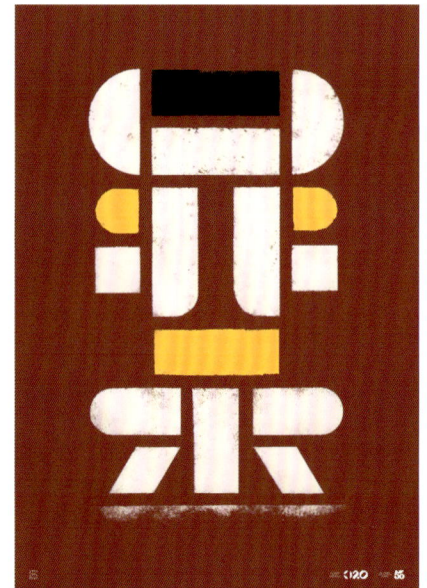

This and following spread:
The twenty Tribler posters
700 × 1000 mm

2014

Silk-screen prints:
Serigraphie Uldry

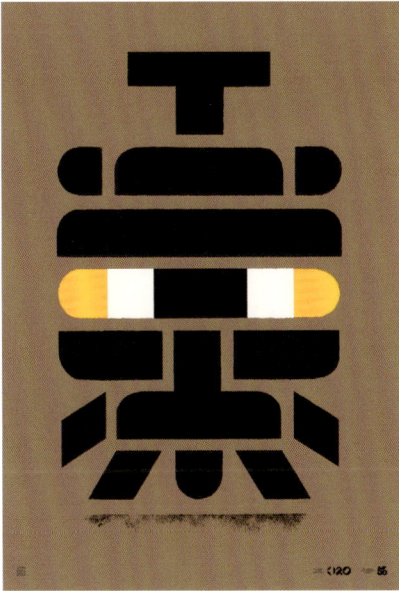
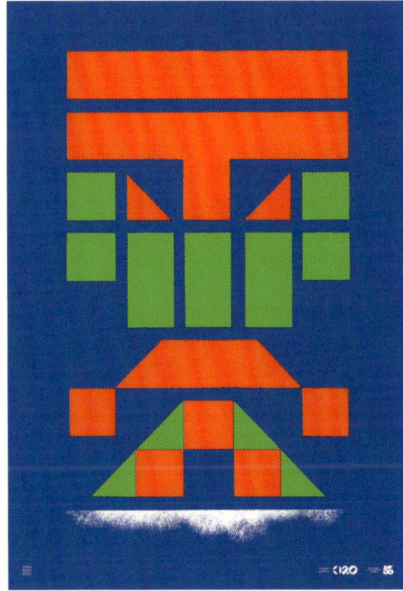
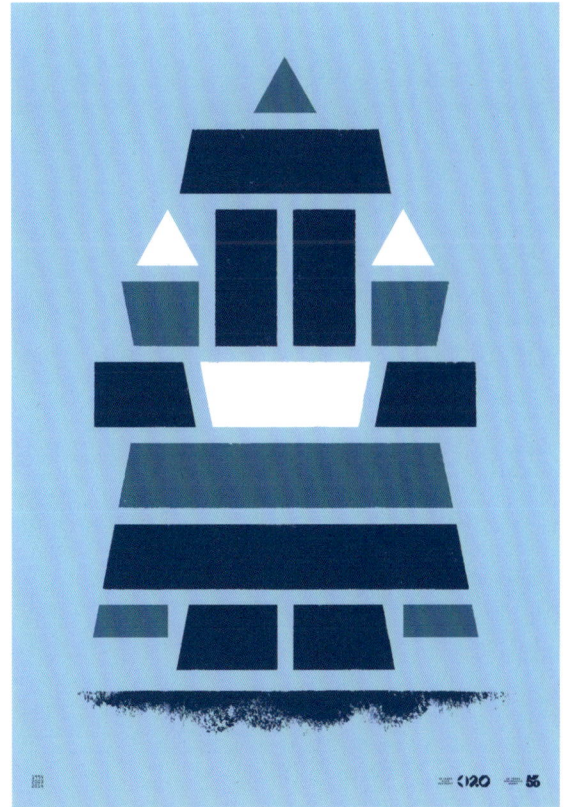
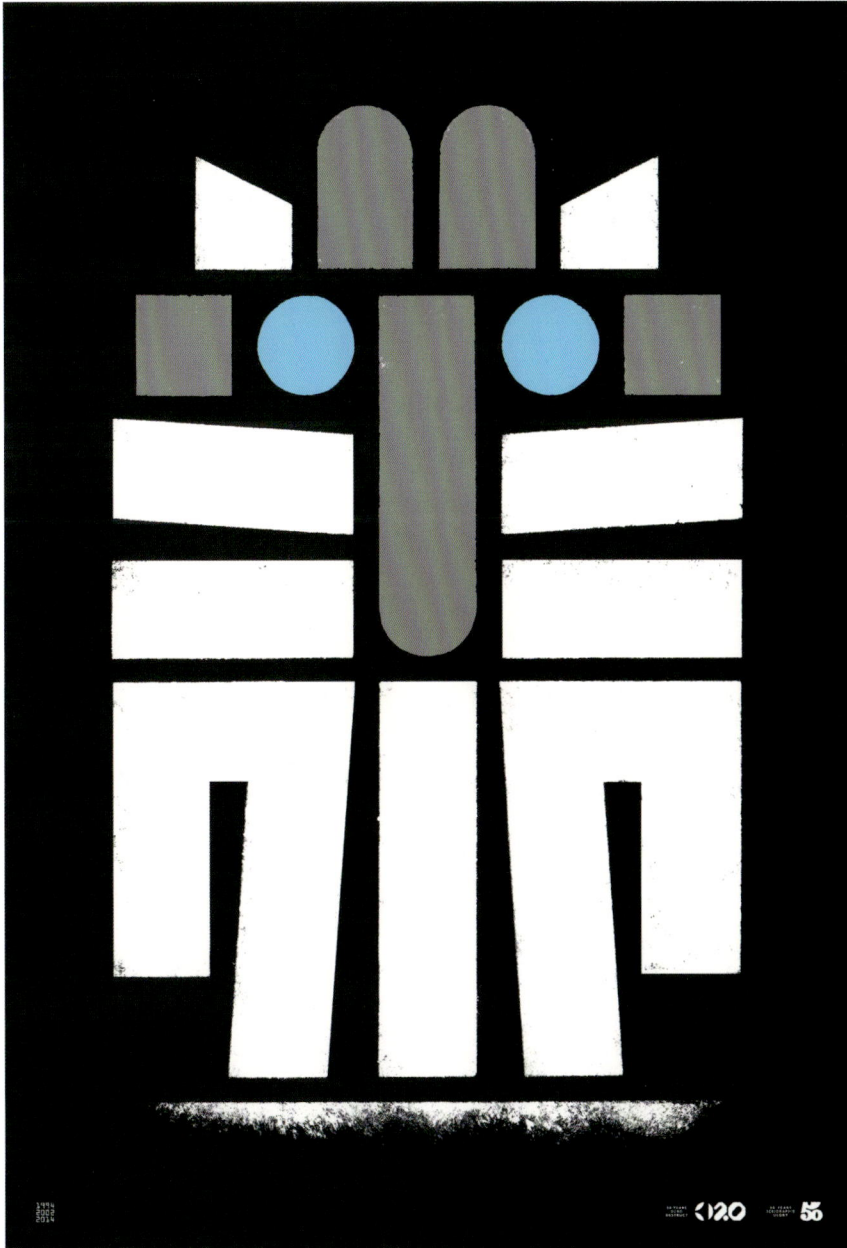

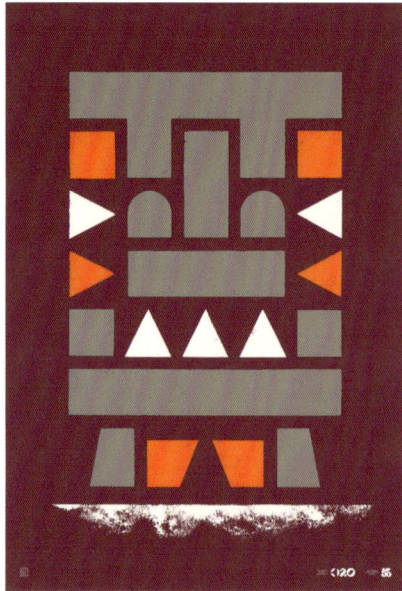

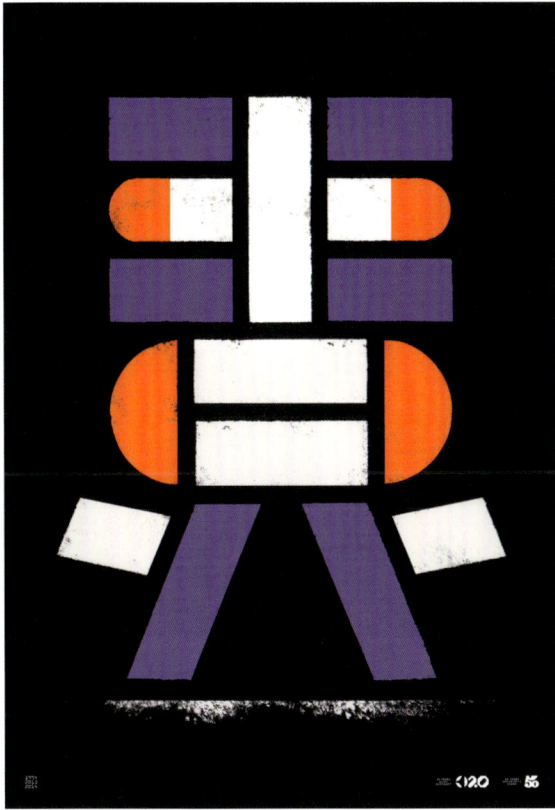

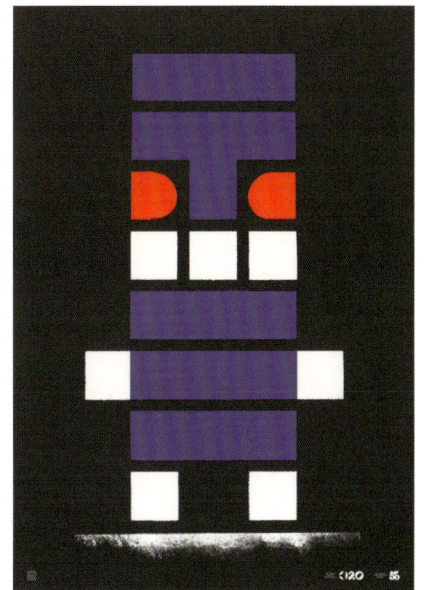

Büro Destruct in Bandung
Lecture, logo-workshop, exhibition and VJ'ing in Bandung, Indonesia.

2013

"Unkl347", "Norrm", "HTH Studio" and "Maja House" invited Büro Destruct to Bandung, Indonesia for a series of events labelled under our motto "Small City – Big Design".

It started with a lecture and a panel discussion at the Maya House, followed by an exhibition with exclusive BD products at the Unkl347 flagship-store, a Büro Discotec with Indonesian Dj's and BD visuals. A logotype workshop with Indonesian students rounded up the very peaceful days with the wonderful people of Bandung!

8ung BanDung!
We will visit you again.

8ung Ban Dung.

Thanks to:

Keni Soeriaatmadja
Ardo Ardhana
Eddi Brokoli
Dendy Darman
Lucas Widiantara
Ipin Arifin Windarman
Anli Rizandi
Egga Pratama
Cworkshope
Morris and Oslo

Unkl
Logotype redesign

Client:
Unkl347, Bandung

2014

Unpublished

Büro Destruct Logotype Workshop "Re-Constructing the Unkl347 Logo".

IT'S NO MASTER PLAN

but these are eight reasonable steps for the creation of a logotype.

©BD 2013, 25.11/v.1.1

1: UNDERSTAND

Understand the client, their philosophy, style, character, products and targets.

2: FEEL

Feel the sound of the brand's wording, loudness, boldness, roundness… Imagine a descriptive picture, a visual.

3: FAMILIARIZE

Familiarize with the word's letters, draw them uppercase, lowercase, play. Sketch the visual ideas (use paper & pencil). Never underestimate your first intention, feeling, idea and visual image. Bring it to paper, no matter how obvious it is.

4: WAIT

Take a break "Let it grow" – one day, one week, just as the deadline allows it. Do various other things. We call it the subconscious mind phase.

5: ADD

Come back and pick what you think is still right. Add what came to mind while away.

6: EXPLORE

It's time to break open your treasures. Browse your font library, think of things you've done before. Think of visual impressions. Pick up fonts and try the letters of the name. Space, kern, combine, customize them… Explore, shape it (on paper or computer). At any time, pay attention to mistakes, they may lead you somewhere never thought of before. Surprise yourself. Store the things you tried on file.

7: FOCUS

Step away and return after the break. One day, one week, just as your schedule allows. Focus on what is stronger, your icon- or your type-idea. Focus on a maximum of three directions you're still happy with and enhance them. Think of a responsive usage of the brand: Horizontal, vertical and square for an avatar profile version. A grid is good to have but don't follow it blindly. Cheat subtly. Refine, polish and spend much effort on details. Clean messy data (unnecessary anchor points and shapes) even if they are not visible in the result.

8: TEST

Make the T-Shirt test. Our golden rule is: We are happy with a logo result if we desire to wear it on a T-Shirt. Test it with your partners and friends. If you feel you're not there yet, repeat from step 1, or any other step in between.

STAK07
Poster design
for a sci-fi exhibition.
700×1000mm

2017

STAK08
Poster design
for a sci-fi exhibition.
700 × 1000 mm

2017

ZÜRICH 2014
EUROPEAN ATHLETICS
CHAMPIONSHIPS

EMZH City Festival Zurich
Event visuals for the city
festival at the Sechseläuten-
platz, Zurich during the
"Athletics European Cham-
pionship Zurich 2014".

Client:
Leichtathletik EM 2014 AG,
Perron 8

2014

Above:
Pattern-brushes for the event
visuals made out of elements
from the given Zurich 2014
European Athletics Championships logotype.

DIE KUNSTLERGRUPPE:

«WIR TRÄUMEN DAVON EINE BERÜHMTE KÜNSTLERGRUPPE ZU WERDEN UND NATÜRLICH WOLLEN WIR ETWAS GANZ NEUES MACHEN..»

DER GALERIST:

«HEUTE HABE ICH WOHL EINE WICHTIGE KUNSTRICHTUNG ENTDECKT.»

CECI N'EST PAS UNE PIPE

©WELTSCHMERTZ95

Weltschmertz

The artist group:
We dream of becoming a famous group of artists and of course we want to do something completely new.

The galerist:
Today I have probably discovered an important art movement.

The spectator:
I could do that.

The art critic:
And suddenly this innovation.

1995

DER BETRACHTER:

«DAS KÖNNTE ICH JA AUCH.»

DER KUNSTKRITIKER:

«UND PLÖTZLICH DIESE INNOVATION.»

SENSE
FUL
NON
SENSE

Bureau de Struct

poésie poétique

BD:97

Mani Matter –
Und so blybt no sys Lied
Tribute CD & DLP sleeve
artworks.

Client:
Meret Matter, Zytglogge
Verlag, Bern

2016

Mani Matter's Bernese German chansons remain very popular in the German speaking part of Switzerland, and Matter has a great influence on the dialect music scene in Bern. His songs are frequently covered.

The tribute collection features interpretations by Greis, Lo & Leduc, Baze, Troubas Kater, Evelinn Trouble, Jeans for Jesus, Max Urban & ZeDe, Tim & Puma Mimi, Jürg Halter, Balduin, and many others.

MANI

MATTER

UND
SO
BLYBT
NO
SYS
LIED

マニ マッテル ⚲

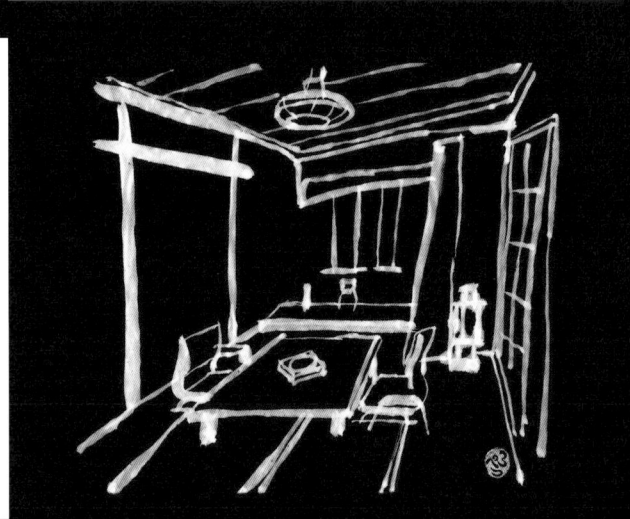

A ryokan (旅館) is a type of traditional Japanese inn that exists since the eighth century. They typically feature tatami-matted rooms, communal baths, and other public areas where visitors may wear yukata (an unlined cotton summer kimono).

Ryokan series
Japanese ink paintings

2011

It was a dark, sleepless and hopeless period. Longing for sleep and rest – the Ryokan series originated at home suffering from a depression during late 2011 until the first light of spring in April 2012.

Lopetz

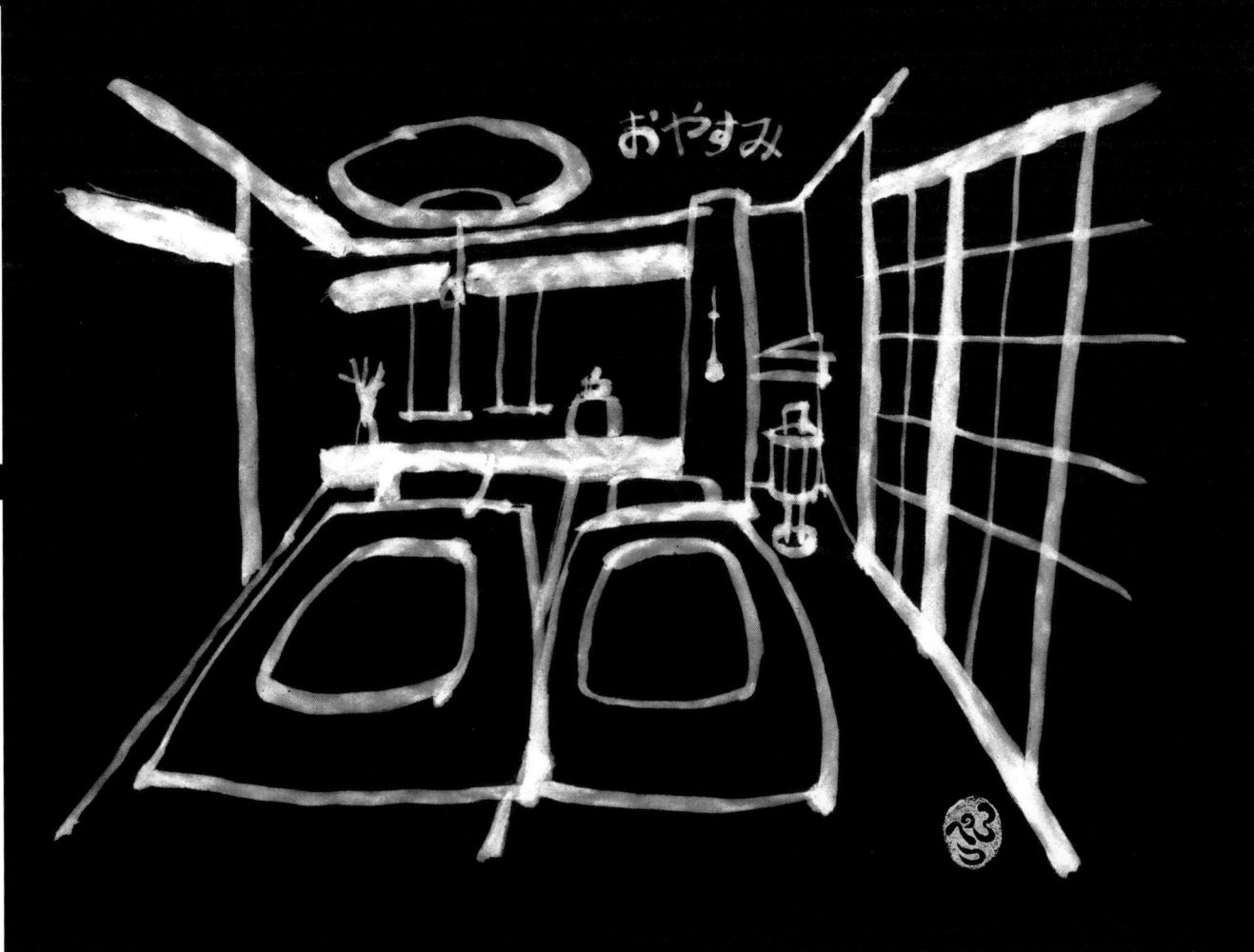

おやすみ

FLVR — flavor

Left page:
FLVR
Logotype porposal

Client:
Eskyflavor, Mickey Eskimo

2020

Unpublished

Kinderfragebuch
Four different cover designs
for Kroegerus & Tschäppeler's
kids question book.

Published by Kein & Aber

Client:
Kein & Aber, Zurich

2012

ISBN 978-3-0369-5661-9

KROGERUS / TSCHÄPPELER
BÜRO DESTRUCT

KiNDER
FRAGEBUCH

KEIN & ABER

KROGERUS / TSCHÄPPELER
BÜRO DESTRUCT

KiNDER
FRAGEBUCH

333 FRAGEN FÜR KINDER IM ALTER VON 7–99 JAHREN

KEIN & ABER

KROGERUS / TSCHÄPPELER
BÜRO DESTRUCT

KiNDER
FRAGEBUCH

KEIN & ABER

KROGERUS / TSCHÄPPELER
BÜRO DESTRUCT

KiNDER
FRAGEBUCH

KEIN & ABER

HiMMEL UND HÖLLE

Schreibe zwei Fragen an Gott
auf einen Zettel. Stecke ihn zusammen
mit einem Rückantwortkuvert
mit deiner Adresse in einen Umschlag.

Jetzt überlege: Wo wohnt Gott?

Vielleicht fragst du deine(n) Lehrer(in)
nach der Adresse. Oder eine(n) Pfarrer(in).
Oder einen anderen Erwachsenen.

Post an Gott von:

DRAUSSEN

Male dieses Bild weiter!

RUND UMS GELD

Wähle ein Kleidungsstück
oder ein Spielzeug aus,
das du nicht mehr magst.

Bring es in einen Secondhand-Laden
und frag, was du dafür noch kriegst.

Verkaufe es, und
schreib den Betrag hier auf.

iN DER SCHULE

Kennst du den Weg
zu deiner Schule?

Zeichne hier einen Plan auf,
sodass ein Fremder den Weg
von dir zu Hause zu deiner
Schule finden könnte.

Kinderfragebuch
Illustrations and editorial
design for Kroegerus &
Tschäppeler's kids question
book.

Published by Kein & Aber

Client:
Kein & Aber, Zurich

2012

ISBN 978-3-0369-5661-9

Spreads, top left
to bottom right:

Heaven and hell, 136/137
Outside, 64/65
All about money, 42/43
In the school, 68/69
What you don't really need
to know, 82/83

WAS DU NiCHT ALLES WiSSEN MUSST

Beantworte die folgenden
drei Fragen:

1.
Was unterscheidet
den Menschen vom Tier?

2.
Was ist das Internet?

3.
Kann man an nichts
denken?

Jetzt stell
die gleichen Fragen
deiner Lieblingslehrerin
oder deinem Lieblingslehrer.
Vergleiche die Antworten.

Spreads, top left
to bottom right:

Your parents, 20/21
Yes or no, 86/87
Boredom, 100/101
Inside, 58/59
The authors, 174/175

Schreib eine Nachricht an deinen Vater oder an deine Mutter.

Eine Frage oder einen Wunsch.

Klebe den Zettel an einen Ort, wo er garantiert gefunden wird.

DEINE ELTERN

Denk dir eine kleine Mutprobe aus, und schreib sie hier hin.

Jetzt lass das Los entscheiden, ob du sie machen musst.

Wirf eine Münze:
Kopf = Du machst es.
Zahl = Du machst es nicht.

JA ODER NEIN

Viele (Erwachsene) mögen Kunst.
Das kann man ganz einfach selber machen.
Besorg dir ein Magazin.
Schneide Bilder aus, die dir besonders gefallen
und klebe sie wild durcheinander
in diesen Bilderrahmen.
Unterschreibe dein Kunstwerk
mit deinem Namen.

LANGEWEILE

Geh zum Fenster
in deinem Zimmer und
schau hinaus.

Was siehst du?

Erstelle eine Liste
von fünf Dingen,
die dir vorher nicht
aufgefallen sind.

DRINNEN

174 AUTOREN 175

Roman Tschäppeler

n° 94 **Hattest du schon mal Heimweh? Wann?**
Als ich in Dänemark studierte, die Sprache noch nicht konnte und meine besten Freunde in der Schweiz vermisste. Da hatte ich fast jeden Tag Heimweh.

n° 93 **Wann und wo hast du zum ersten Mal das Meer gesehen? Wie war das?**
Als ich 6 Jahre alt war und mit meinen Eltern und meinem Bruder in die Bretagne fuhr. Es war sehr kalt und schlammig, ich war etwas enttäuscht.

n° 186 **Nenne drei Dinge, die stinken!**
Der Kühlschrank im Ferienhaus meines Freundes, der Flur des Einwohnermeldeamtes, mein Musikstudio.

Mikael Krogerus

n° 60 **Dein Auto ist:**
geil normal peinlich wir haben keins.
Ein greilroter Golf-Kombi aus dem Jahre 1997. Mein Sohn findet ihn so peinlich, dass es schon fast wieder geil ist.

n° 302 **Wenn du dich heute entscheiden müsstest: Was willst du später werden?**
Michael Lewis.

n° 227 **Mit welchem Witz bringst du fast jeden zum Lachen?**
»Kennst du den? Sagt der eine: Immer wenn ich Kaffee trinke, kann ich nicht schlafen. Sagt der andere: »Komisch, bei mir ist es umgekehrt. Wenn ich schlafe, kann ich keinen Kaffee trinken.?« - »Nein, erzähl mal!«

»Lopetz« Gianfreda, Büro Destruct

n° 111 **Nenne zwei Regeln bei dir zu Hause:**
Regel 1 Beim Eintreten die Schuhe ausziehen,
Regel 2 Eine Münze in das Sparschwein meines Sohnes einwerfen, wenn ich mich nicht an Regel 1 gehalten habe.

n° 296 **Was war früher dein Lieblingsspielzeug?**
Legos.
Was ist es heute?
Logos.

n° 201 **Was ist dein Trick, wenn du nicht einschlafen kannst?**
Ein Glas kalte Milch trinken, manchmal noch ein, zwei Kekse dazu.

Year 2000
20 years Reitschule
leporello

Client:
Reitschule, Bern

2017

BD:106

REGULAR

CONDENSED

EXTENDED

R R R R

BD MICRON_FONT
VARIABLE TYPEFACE
EXTENDED
@2348/
R£$.×

BD MICRON_FONT
VARIABLE TYPEFACE
REGULAR
@0123456789/
R£$#%£!@@@£N?.×

BD MICRON_FONT
VARIABLE TYPEFACE
CONDENSED
@0123456789/R£
$V£#%£!@@@£NV?.×

AAAAAAÆBCÇDDE
ÉÉÉÉFGHIIIJKLM
NÑOÒÓ ÔÕ ÖØŒPPQ
RSTUÙ ÚÛ ÜVWW
WXY Ý ÿZ À Á
ÄÅ ÆBCÇDDEÉ
ÉÉÉFGHIIIJKLMNÑ
OÒÓ ÔÕ ÖØŒ PPQRS
RTUÙ ÚÛ ÜVWWW
WXY Ý ÿZ01234
56789/!!?¿.—●×╫/
/^()[]——«»»‹‹‹
›"""&§£¢¥+—×÷=×
~?@®™©°º|.,::

BD MicronFont
Variable font with 5 instances
Condensed, Semi-Condensed,
Regular, Semi-Extended,
Extended.

2019

www.typedifferent.com

BD:107

Technoculture 2 [Man-Machine] is the second edition of an exhibition testing the limits of art, music and technology in the Halle Grise of the former Cardinal Brewery, now blueFACTORY, in Fribourg, Switzerland. Over a period of 13 weeks (25/5– 11/8/2019), les Archives du Futur Antérieur presented a programme ranging from exhibitions, original artistic productions, parties, performances, concerts, film screenings, to talks and kid's activities. We were asked by curator Adrien Laubscher to come up with a visual identity for the project. We created two variable fonts to cover the multiple demands – one for the titles and one featuring the robot characters called the "Microns". The simple, technical yet playful graphic language in black and white allowed us to design large banners, posters, flags, flyers, event-banners, stencils, merchandise and videos for social media within a limited timeframe and production budget. A call for entries was put out to a hundred artists two months before the opening. Ten projects were also asked and produced. One of them was the creation of stencils based on BD fonts and Microns, which were spray-painted on the walls inside and outside of the building. BD was also asked to contribute to the titling of "In C", a short film of the opening night musical performance by The Young Gods and La Landwehr released in 2021. In 1998, the late curator Michel Ritter invited us to contribute to Technoculture 1 [Computerworld] at the Fri-Art Kunsthalle. In 2019 the Technoculture mothership landed in the iconic Cardinal warehouse, a monument of the city's industrial architecture heritage. The 2500 sm hall was transformed into a horizontal cathedral, functioning as a laboratory, a mystical space and a time machine, all in one. Live events were organized on the weekends, with the public surrounded by the artworks. Les Archives du Futur Antérieur took up the challenge to produce the exhibition in less than 5 months, allowing the spaceship to once more take off. The optimistic take of 1998, which focused on the general association of art and technology, gave way in 2019 to a more dystopian view of technology, raising questions about the actual relationship between humans and machines. The third edition of Technoculture is planned for 2040.

Adrien Laubscher,
Les Archives du Futur Antérieur

Micron Robots Stencils
20 stencils were sprayed all over the Technoculture 2 Festival location at the former Cardinal brewery in Fribourg.

Sprayed by
Mathis Baltisberger

2019

BD MicronRobots

BD MicronRobots
Variable font featuring 52
Micron characters.

www.typedifferent.com

2019

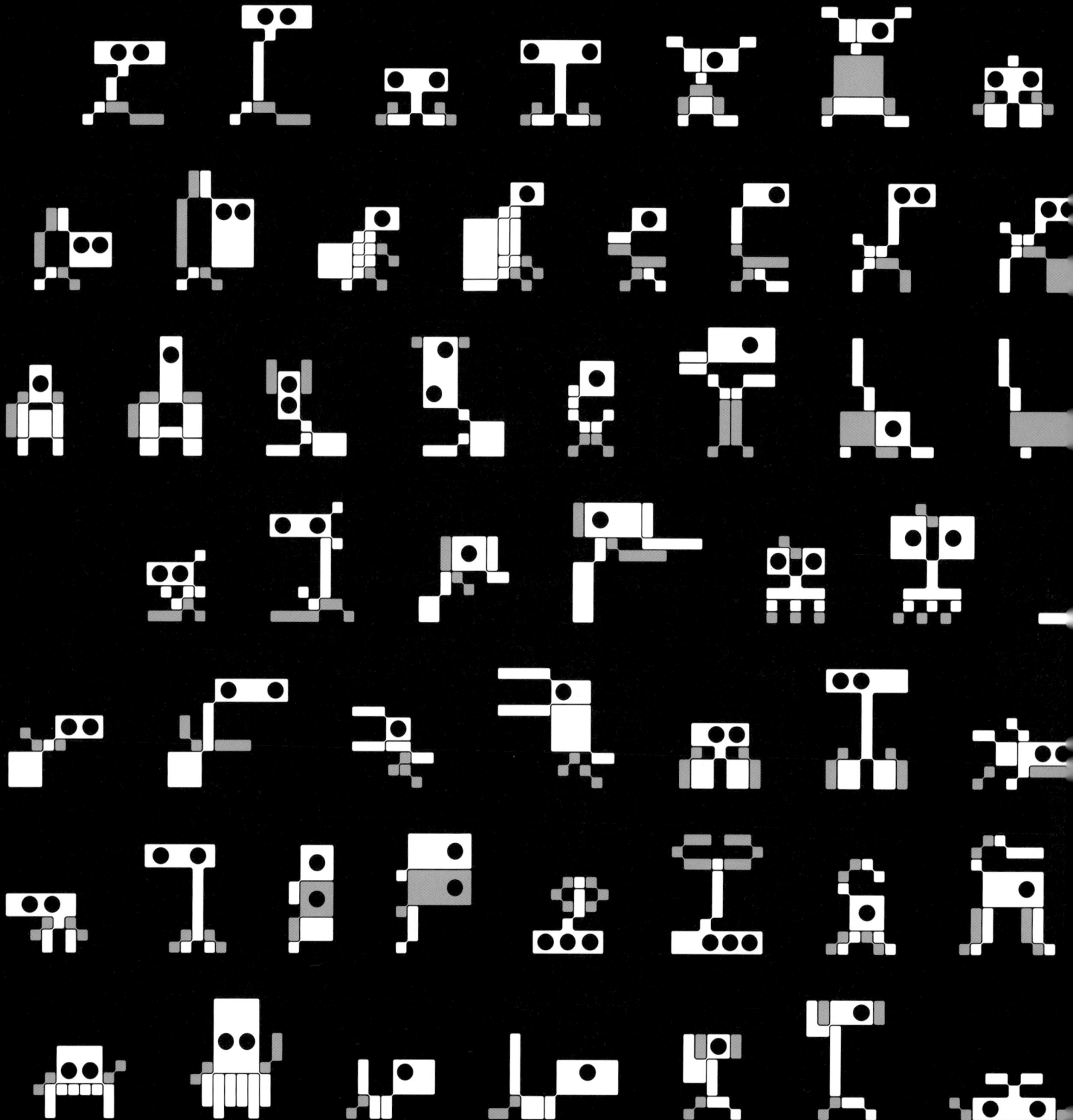

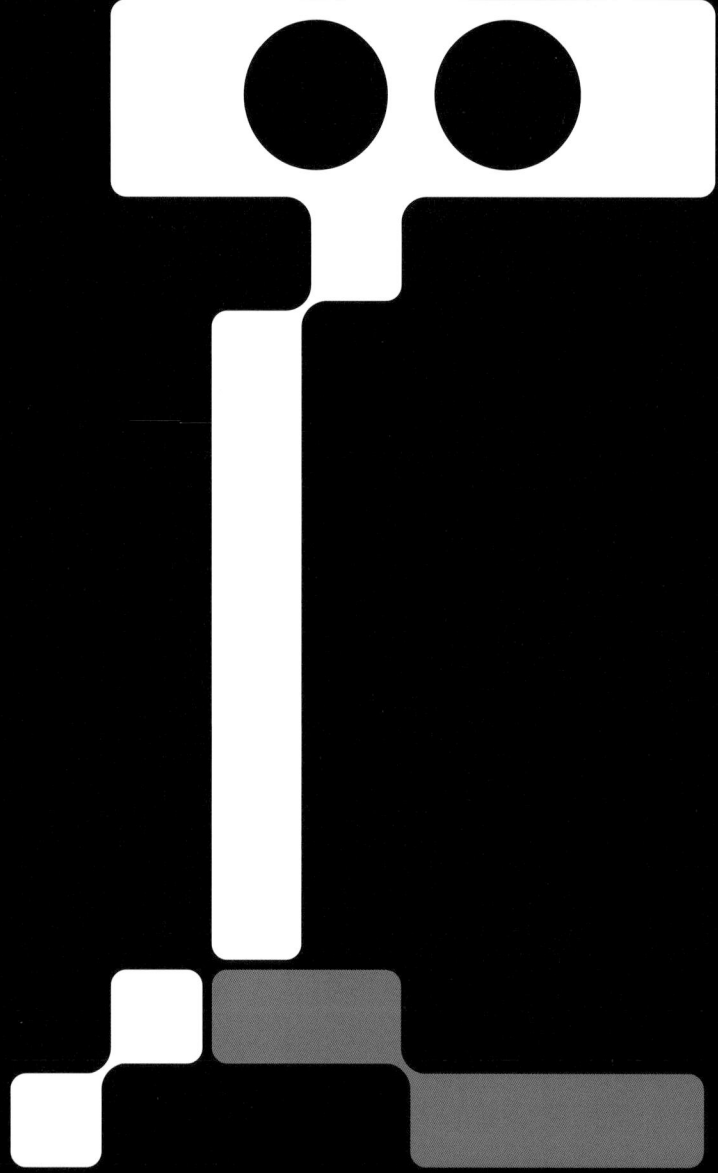

Technoculture Rebirth
Poster
420 × 594 mm

Client:
Archives du Futur
Antérieur, blueFactory,
Fribourg

2017

TECHNOCULTURE
REBIRTH

15.12.2018
STARTS 22:00
ENTRY CHF 10.-

blueFACTORY
PASSAGE DU CARDINAL 1, FRIBOURG
ARCHIVESDUFUTURANTERIEUR.NET

>HOSTED BY GRETA GRATOS
>DRAG RACE BY GENEVEGAS
>TECHNO MUSIC BY LA BOHÈME, NIN
>VISUALS BY GERTRUDE TUNING

ammonit events & DUBQUEST PRESENTS

The Kruder &

REITSCHULE BERN
GROSSE HALLE
SAT. 26
SEPT. 09
10PM – 6AM

FEAT
MCs RAS T-WEED
& EARL ZINGER

VISUALS
FRITZ FRITZKE

SUPPORT
MAKOSSA & MEGABLAST
JAY SANDERS

Dorf meister Session

EXCLUSIVE SWISS SHOW 2009
PRESALE starticket

DECO BY TEXTILINSTALLATION.CH   trans form TEXTIL_INSTALLATION

VALSER SKYY RONERO kulturagenda cbm PARTY NEWS. hero dance passive attack OLMO CHAIR maha ooga SUCCESS Vino della Casa

**The Kruder & Dorfmeister
Session**
Concert poster and flyer
420 × 594 mm
105 × 210 mm

Client:
Ammonit Events,
DubQuest

2009

Papyrus Plike Paper
A bizarre booklet, presenting an intergalactic document of terrestrial hieroglyphs printed on the Plike paper range by Papyrus.

240×170 mm, 12 pages

Client:
Visionandfactory,
Papyrus Europe, Belgium

2011

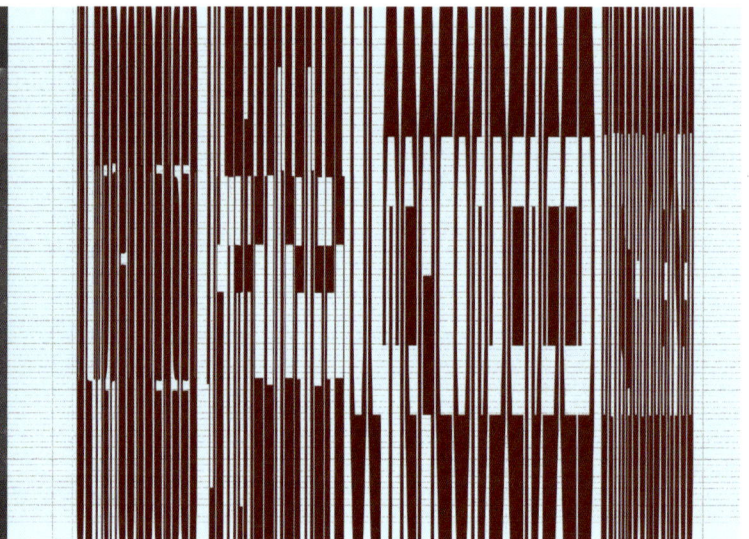

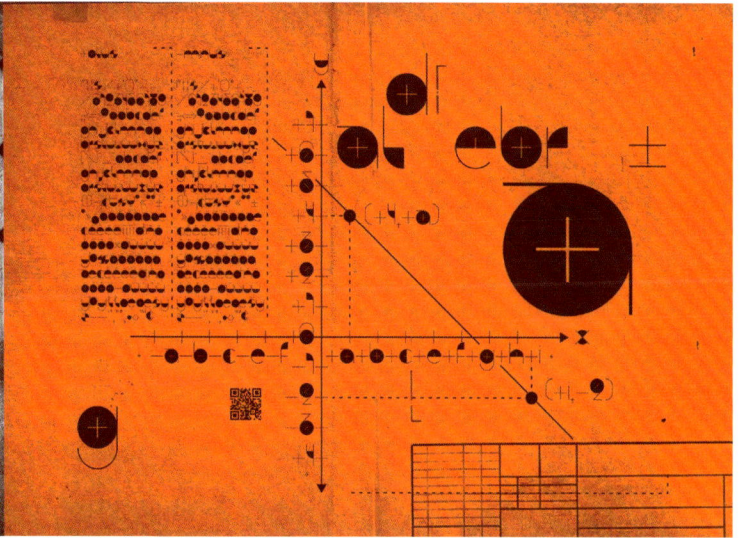

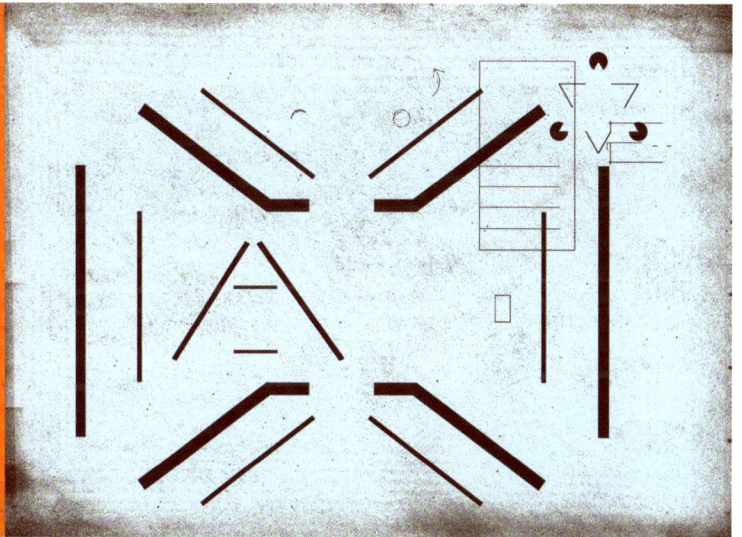

Vectorworks Architektur
Image campaign drafts for a
Vectorworks CAD software
promotion.

Client:
Computerworks,
Vectorworks, Zurich

2011

Unpublished

Top left:
ZHdK, Toni Areal, Zurich
by EM2N Architekten AG.

Top right:
New Monte Rosa Hut
by Studio Monte Rosa
at the ETH Zurich's
architecture & construction
department.

Bottom:
Vector cities.

Right page:
House in Binningen
by Luca Selva Architekten.

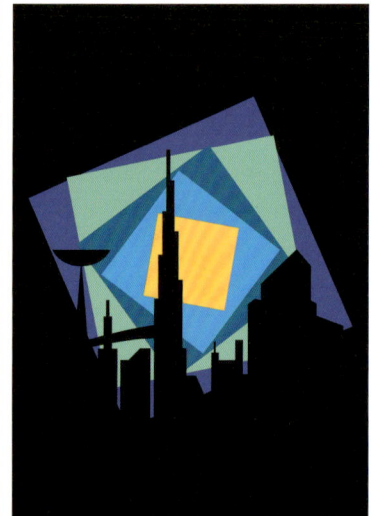

Schauspielhaus Zürich
Concept, art direction and editorial design of season 2015/16 book.

Photos: Lieblinge

Cover photo: Luc Viatour

Client:
Schauspielhaus Zürich

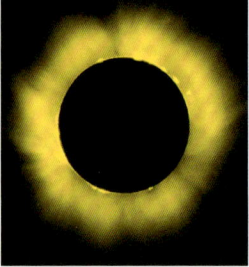

2015

The theater ensemble photos were inspired by legendary album covers.

Top left to bottom right:
Robert Hunger-Bühler, Klaus Brömmelmeier, Susanne-Marie Wrage, Frederike Wagner,

Julia Kreusch, Ludwig Boettger, Nicolas Rosat, Michel Neuenschwander, Matthias Neukirch, Isabelle Menke, Elisa Plüss, Hilke Altefrohne, Sofia Elena Borsani, Nils Kahnwald, Michael Maertens, Benedict Fellmer, Gottfried Breitfuss.

Signs, Symbols, Icons, Type
Findings from all around the
globe – posted regularly on
Instagram.

Since 2010

@BuroDestruct

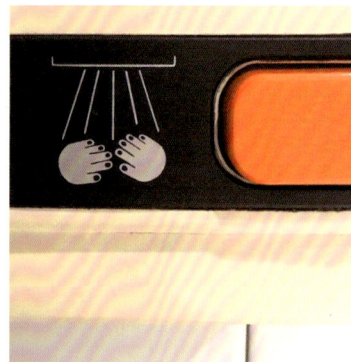

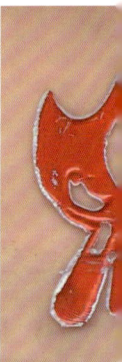

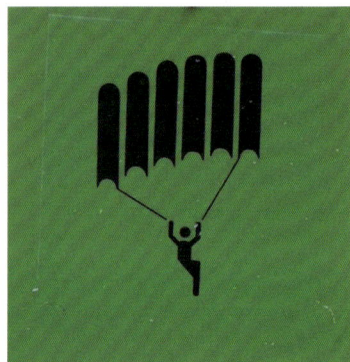

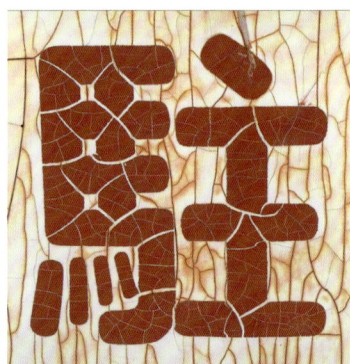

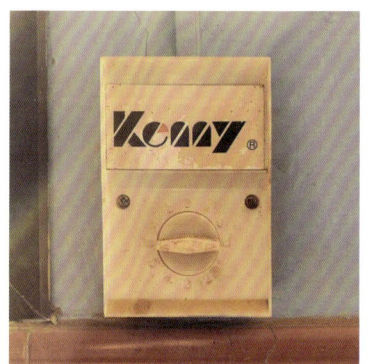

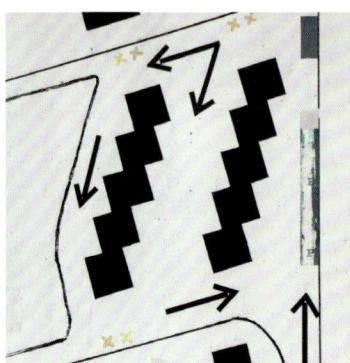

ATL

BD

Hüt isch FONDUE Wätter

GLEIS !

ISO 3098/I   DIN 6776
ISO   Bv **10,0** mm
m̄   Ψ **1,0** mm
Art. 342 100

フランス菓子 ドンク 六甲アイランド 工場
フランス菓子 ドンク 六甲アイランド 工場
フランス菓子 ドンク 六甲アイランド 工場
フランス菓子 ドンク 六甲アイランド 工場
フランス菓子 ドンク 六甲アイランド 工場
フランス菓子 ドンク 六甲アイランド 工場

NORMALUZ
LUMINISCENTE
CLASE B 10/15
RD00116
UNE 23035/4
60/5,6-800 K   W
D<10 m.

COFFEE·HOUSE
fong
椎名町店 tel 3973—5196
池袋西口店 tel 3982—4280

LR

あぶない！
きゅうに、ふかくなっています。
Deep water ahead.

100 T

Bomb The Bass
CD & LP sleeve artworks for
the "Back to Light" album and
single releases "The Infinites",
"Boy / Girl", "Up The
Mountain", "X-Ray Eyes"
and the "Back To Light – FM
Radio Gods Remix Collection".

Published by !K7

Client:
Tim Simenon, UK

2010

BTB Logomark 2010

BTB Logomark 2011

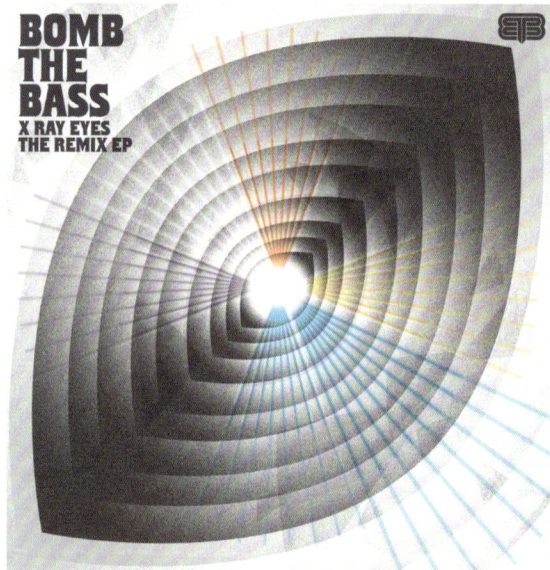

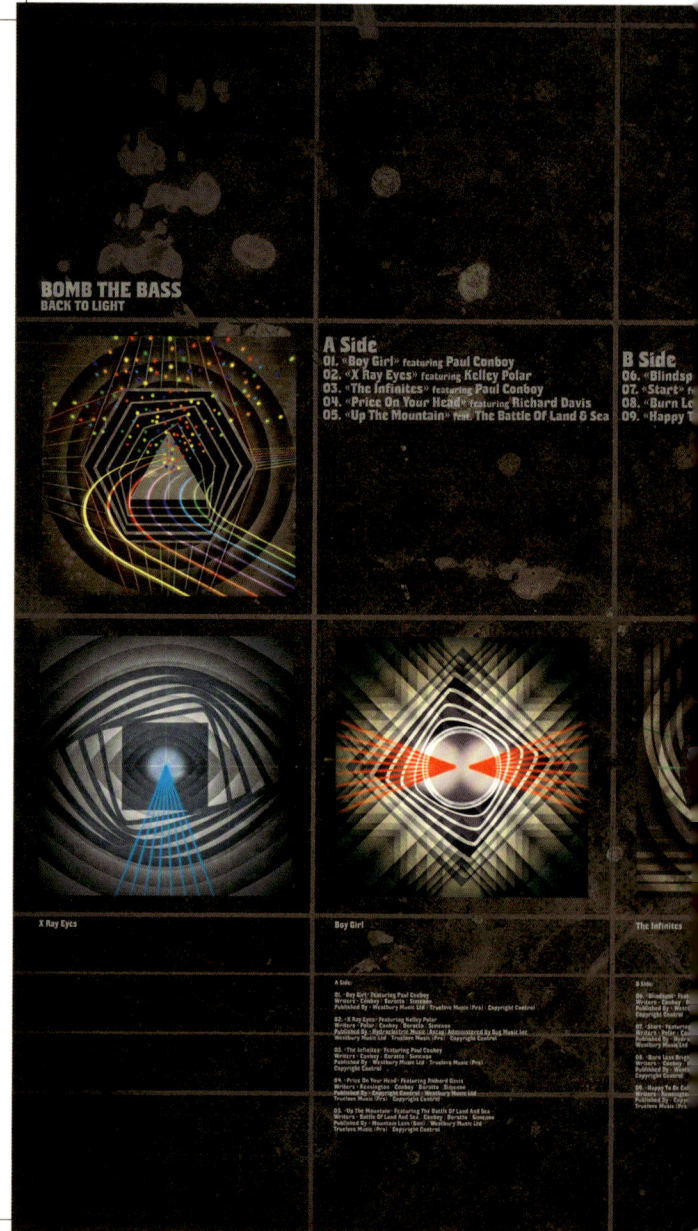

Early artwork versions

Unpublished

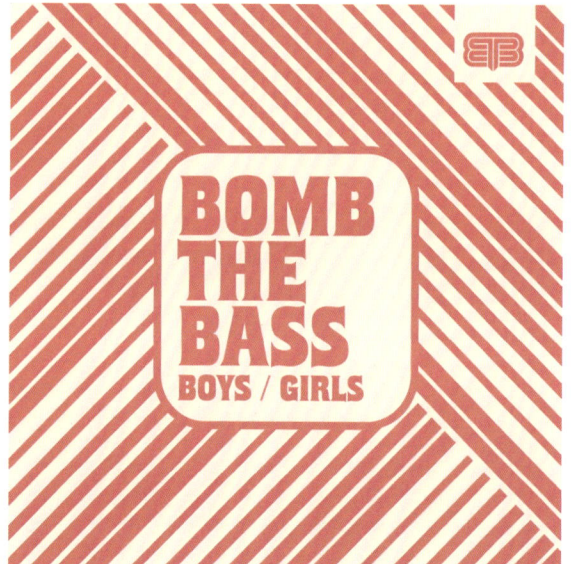

BD:122

BOMB THE BASS
BACK TO LIGHT

Production: Tim Simenon, Paul Conboy And Gui Boratto
Mix: Tim Simenon With Fopac Talman At Vintage Audio
Mastering: Simon Francis At Masterpiece
Cover: Live Drums Recorded At Mosh São Paulo
Additional Outro Backing Vocal Sample On "Start": Rodrigo Rossi
Sleeve Optics: Lopetz10: Buro Destruct

Paul Conboy
chard Davis

Up The Mountain

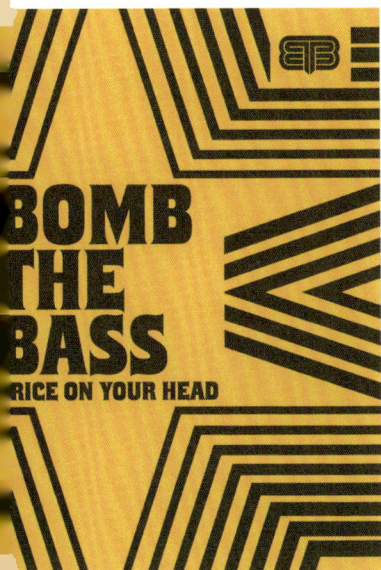

BOMB
THE
BASS
RICE ON YOUR HEAD

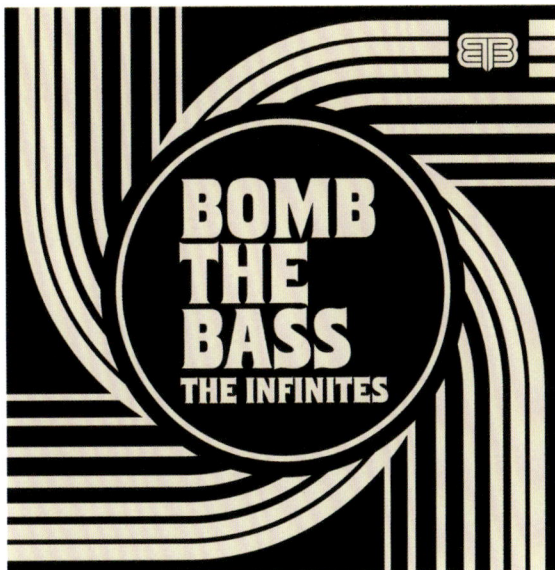

BOMB
THE
BASS
THE INFINITES

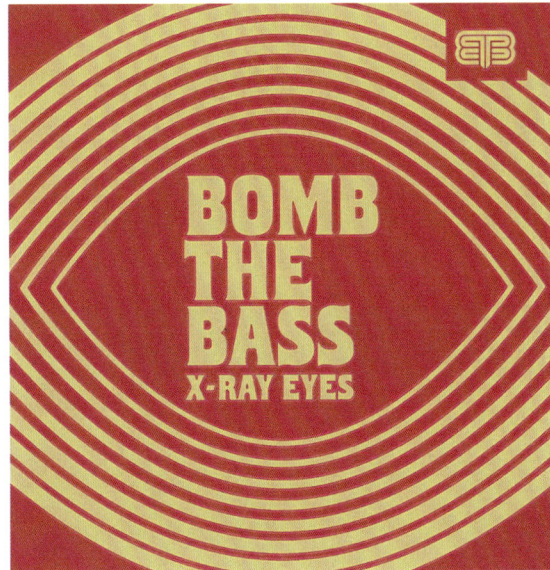

BOMB
THE
BASS
X-RAY EYES

BD:123

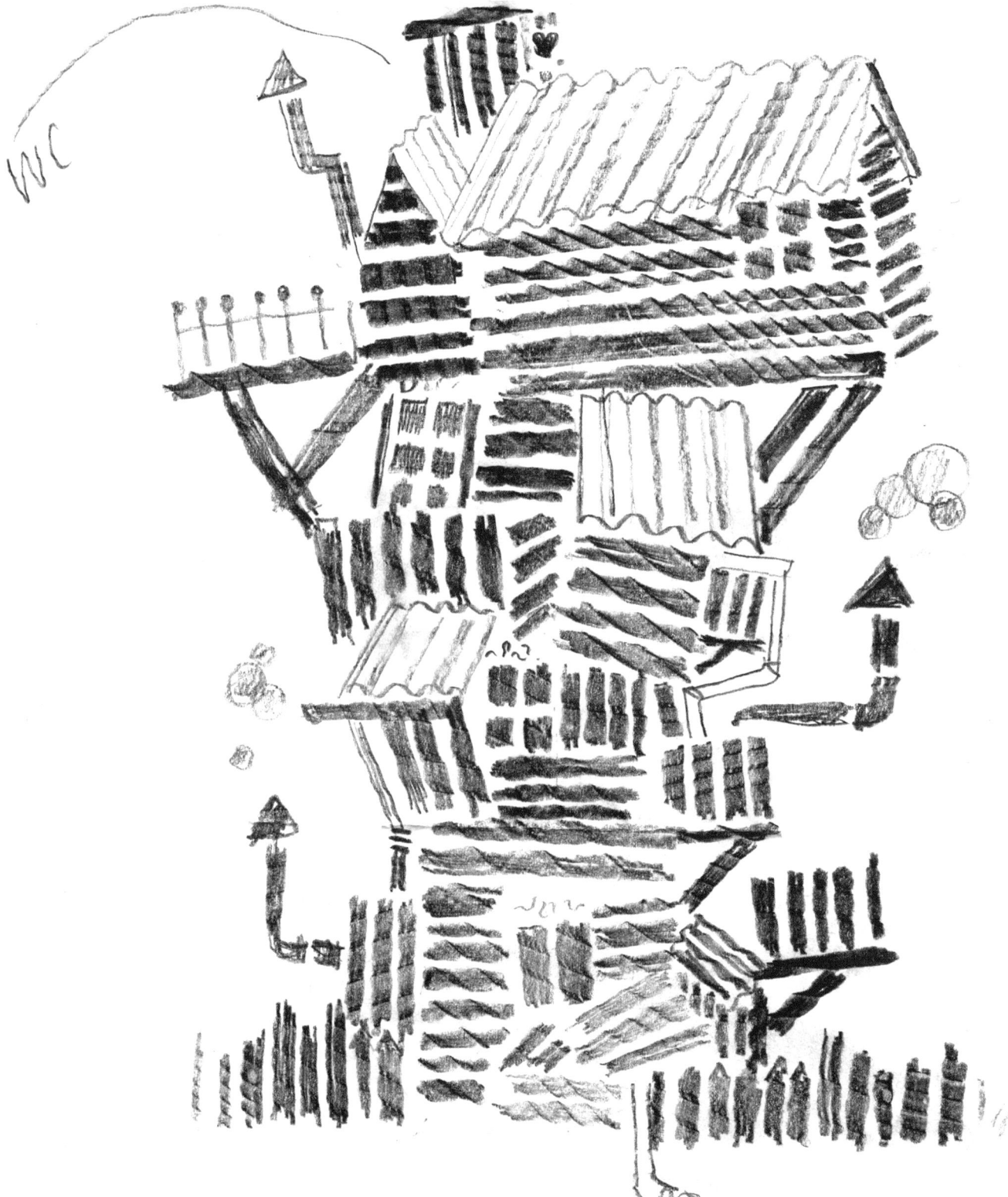

Cha Cha Dacha

TAKE
A

EAK

Bureau de Struct
connaisseurs de récréation

BERLIN
BY BÜRO DESTRUCT

KREUZBERG

MITTE

TACHELES

SCHÖNEBERG

A sabbatical in Berlin
Working on various 20th anniversary Büro Destruct projects, such as a new BD website, BD icon(s), typeface, poster series ideas ...

Spring 2013

MAUERPARK

PRENZLAUER BERG

Berlin 11.06.2013

SPANDAU

BD:126

Top and bottom:
"BD Icon", "BD 20 Years Büro
Destruct" and evolution of the
"BD Tanga Icon".

2013

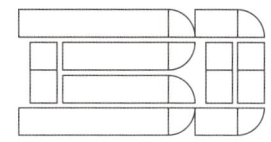

CHARLOTTENBURG

BD Pankow
Typedifferent font
(Formerly named BD Berlin).

2013

www.typedifferent.com

PANKOW

BD BERLIN

AABCDEFGHHIJKLMNOOPQ
QRSTUVWXYZ 0123456789#
$Ø¥¢£ $?!ff BℓQ ©®™
ÑÎÙÒÇŽÜŒŒÅØQ|ÞÐŁ[«.+;–._/
'*'%×"='''\±%.÷|'ⲅ{₉₉{₉°'ᵇᵇ~"]

20 YEARS
BÜRO
DESTRUCT

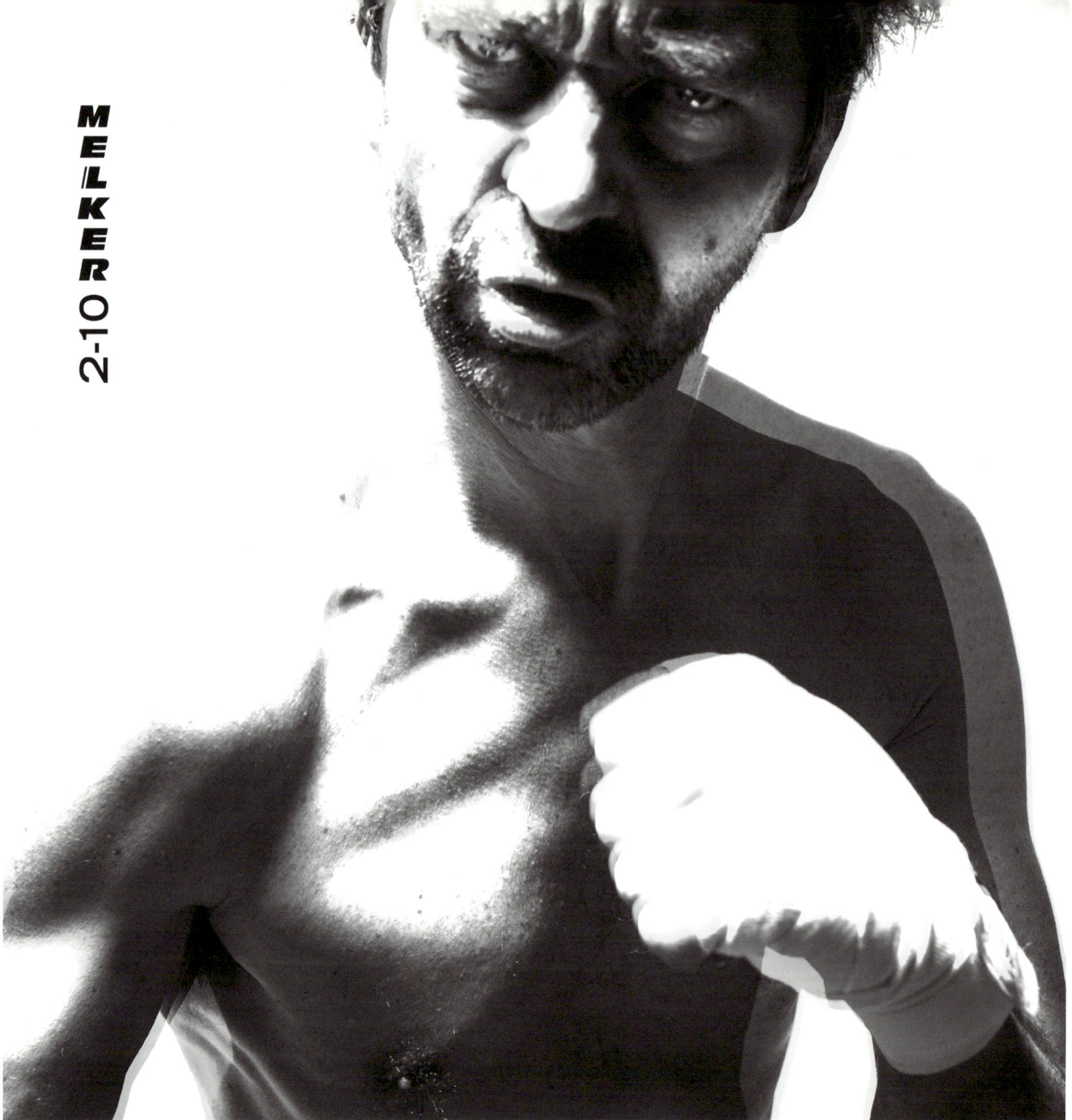

MELKER

2-10

Melker
Logotype, LP sleeve artwork
and concert poster design.
420 × 594 mm

Photo: Simon Opladen

Published by Warmer Brother
Recordings

Client: Melker

2017

MELKER

2-10

A
1 Tiffany
2 Trip
3 Chaut wi is
4 1. Stock
5 Schlazug
6 Vide

B
1 Robin H
2 Reality
3 Monbijou
4 Hermrige
5 Dini Fründin
6 Du kensches

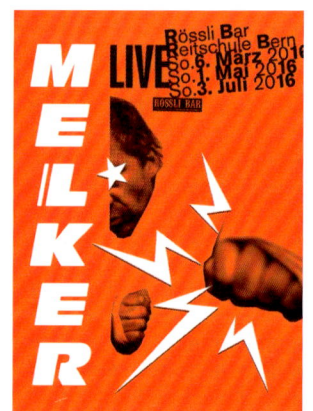

Logofolia

KULTARENA®
EVENTHALLE

Centraldubs

HOTEL KOSMOS

FREI LUFT

SWISS GAMES

Digital Play-ground.

2013
Eidgenössisches Turnfest
Fête fédérale de gymnastique
Biel Bienne

Gymnastique Fantastique

Top left to bottom right: "Passtricot", Client: Passtricot, 2016 / "Galaxy Gerd", Client: Neue Freunde, 2017 / "Foundation Award", Client: Computerworks AG, 2010 / "Terra Vecchia", Client: Stiftung Terra Vecchia, 2012 / "Glasfasernetz Schweiz", Client: Furrer.Hugi&Partner, 2011 / "Nova Zona", Client: Nova Zona, VR Marketing & Entertainment, 2017 / "TWB", Client: Thomas Weibel, 2011 / "Humantools", Client: Kaspar Lüthi, 2018 / "Cosplay Festival Bern", Client: Cosplay Festival, 2017 / "Perfect Circuit", Client: Perfect Circuit, 2018 / "Bamako Bar", Client: Zera Huber, 2018 / "Schnapswerk", Client: Schnapswerk, 2013 / "Ajojespa", Client: Ajoiespa, Spa Lounge Living, 2013

Next page, top left to bottom right: "Momobil", Client: Ferenz Poor, 2019 / "Vocalism", Client: Lodel Fizler, 2002 / "Retrospekt", Client: Retrospekt GmbH, 2019 / "KPT", Client: KPT Krankenkasse AG, 2015 / "Lomotion", Client: Lomotion AG, 2018 / "Learning from Tokyo", Client: Hosoya Schaefer Architects, 2011 / "Dadarchitekten", Client: dadarchitekten gmbh, 2011 / "Yokai", Client: Michael Zumstein, 2013

momobil

vocalism

Retrospekt

kpt:

LOMOTION

dadarchitekten

YOKAI

TOKYO FROM LEARNING

Top left to bottom right: "Bunq Inn", Client: bunq Architectes FAS, 2019 / "Animativ", Client: Jérôme Blum, 2015 / "MixUp!", Client: Dampfzentrale & Schlachthaus Theater Bern, 2016 / "Kargo", Client: Kargo Kommunikation GmbH, 2010 / "Alte Feuerwehr Viktoria", Client: Genossenschaft Feuerwehr Viktoria, 2015 / "Vision-E", Client: Christoph Bürki, 2016 / "Best Of Iceland", Client: Marianne Wittwer, 2016 / "auawirleben", Client: auawirleben Theaterfestival Bern, 2018 / "Öffentlichkeitsgesetz.ch", Client: Öffentlichkeitsgesetz, 2011 / "Geisha", Client: Jacqueline Wehrle, 2018 / "Continent Club", Client: Christoph Bürki, 2018 / "Mobilkran", Client: Mobilkran AG, 2013 / "Out+About", Client: Internationales Theaterfestival Bümpliz-Bethlehem, 2016

Top left to bottom right: "Dub Colony", Client: Dub Colony, 2019 / "Time To Move", Client: Time for Change, 2019 / "Creative Hub", Client: Creative Hub, 2019 / "Wobmann", Client: Wobmann & Partner AG, 2014 / "Maximizerz", Client: Maximizers, 2014 / "Google", 2021 / "Naos Architekten", Client: Naos Architekten, 2021 / "Connected", Client: LMVZ, Lehrmittelverlag Zürich, 2017 / "Supergraff", Client: Silver Worldwide Ventures LLC, 2017 / "Hänsel & Gretel", Client: Coiffure Hänsel & Gretel, 2014 / "Mütter- und Väterberatung", Client: Mütter- und Väterberatung Kanton Bern, 2016 / "Oasis", Client: Palais-Galerie, 2021 / "Cividi", Client: Hosoya Schaefer Architects, 2019

DUB COLONY

TIME TO MOVE →

creative hub

WOBMANN & PARTNER AG

MAXIMIZERZ

google

NAOS Architekten

connected
Medien und Informatik

SUPERGRAFF

coiffure
HÄNSEL & GRETEL

MÜTTER- UND
VÄTERBERATUNG
KANTON BERN

オアシス

cividi

Top left to bottom right: "Batkovic", Client: Mario Batkovic, 2020 / "Gaian", Client: Zero Point Energy Inc., 2019 / "Prostata Records", Client: Prostata Records, 2019 / "vierXfünf", Client: vierXfünf Gartendesign, 2020 / "Musikschule Köniz", Client: Musikschule Köniz, 2020 / "Solvas", Client: Solvas Advokatur, Notrariat, Mediation, 2016 / "Soft Electronics", Client: Jaro Gielens, 2020 / "JMO", Client: Jan Galega Brönnimann, 2016 / "Equapack", Client: Equapack Inc., 2020 / "Könizer", Client: Gemeinde Köniz, 2020 / "Slash Production", Client: Slash Production, 2013 / "Bächtelen", Client: Stiftung Bächtelen, 2008

MiniChef
MiniChef cooks and distributes
a healthy, fresh and handmade
organic baby porridge for little
people.

Client:
MiniChef, Dani Rolli

2019

Gulasch Guschti
Gulasch Guschti cooks
and serves spicy Hungarian
goulash. Also for vegans.

Client:
Ferenz Poor

2020

All elements used on the
artwork for "Alphatronic –
Sonic Landscapes".

2009

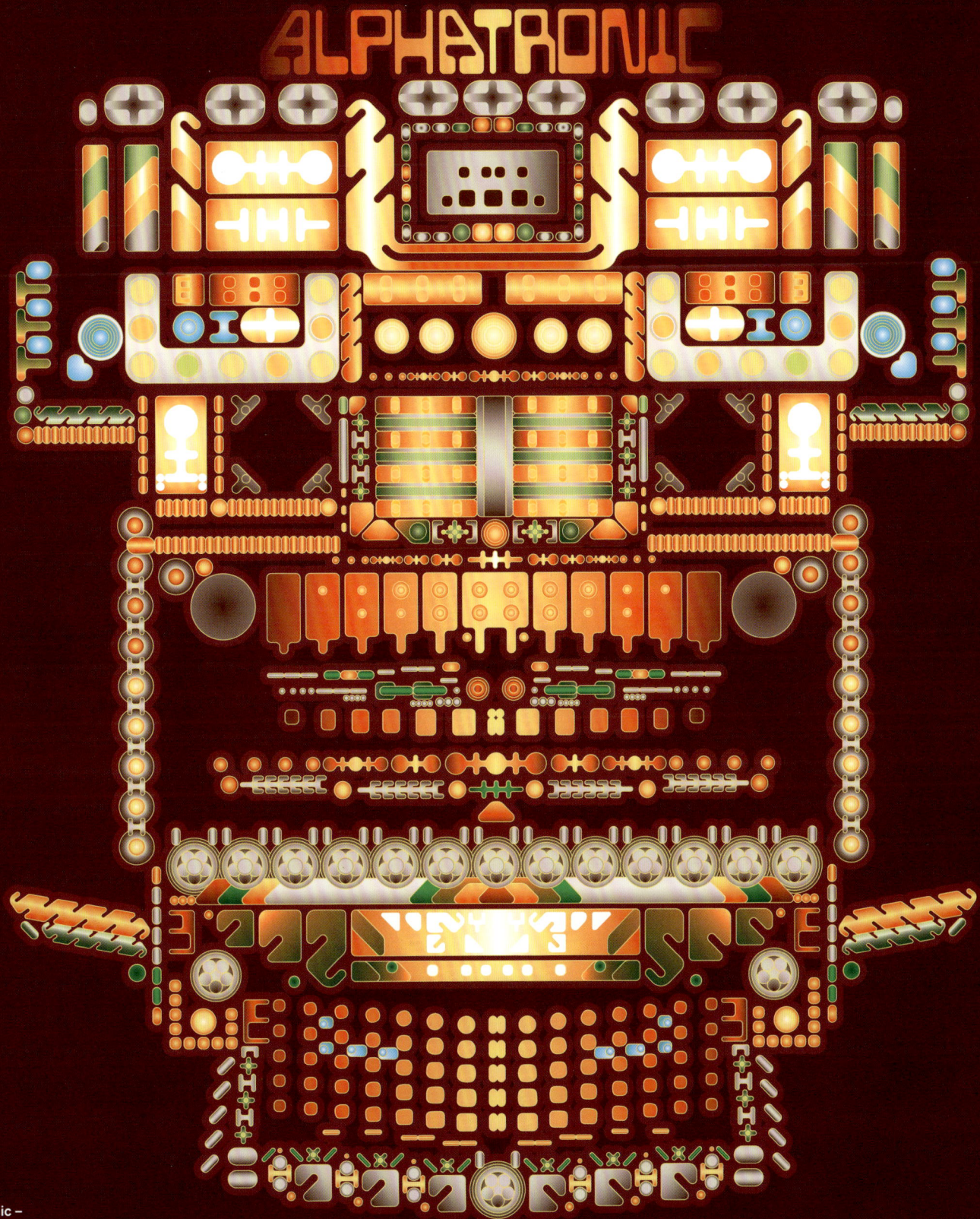

**Alphatronic –
Sonic Landscapes**
CD sleeve artwork

Published by Everest Records

Client:
Daniel Wihler, Alphatronic

2009

Alphatronic – Cybersyn
LP sleeve artwork

Published by Everest Records

Client:
Daniel Wihler, Alphatronic

2011

BD:138

ALPHATRONIC

TECHNICO ELECTRIC

Alphatronic – Technico
Electric
CD & EP sleeve artwork

Published by Everest Records

Client:
Daniel Wihler, Alphatronic

2016

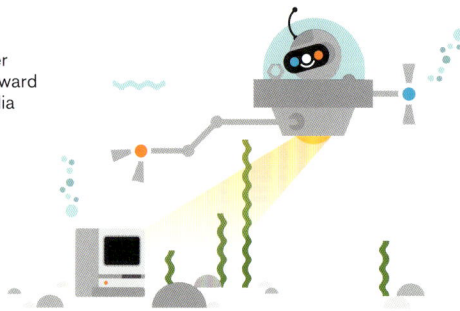
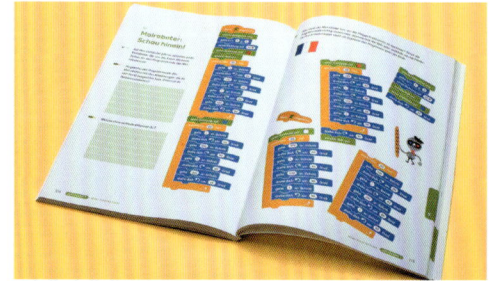

Connected Vol. 1–4
Illustrations and character-
design of textbooks for schoolkids learning and understanding
media and informatics.

Client:
LMVZ Lehrmittelverlag Zürich

Editorial design:
In co-operation with Etage Est

Photos: Rolf Siegenthaler

Published by
LMVZ Lehrmittelverlag Zürich

1: ISBN 978-3-03713-776-5
2: ISBN 978-3-03713-777-2
3: ISBN 978-3-03713-778-9
4: ISBN 978-3-03713-779-6

2017–2021

Awards:
Worlddidac Award Winner
& Swisscom Innovation Award
2020, Comenius EduMedia
Siegel 2019

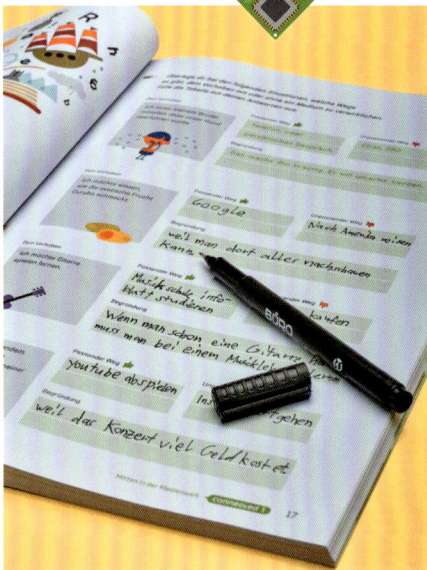

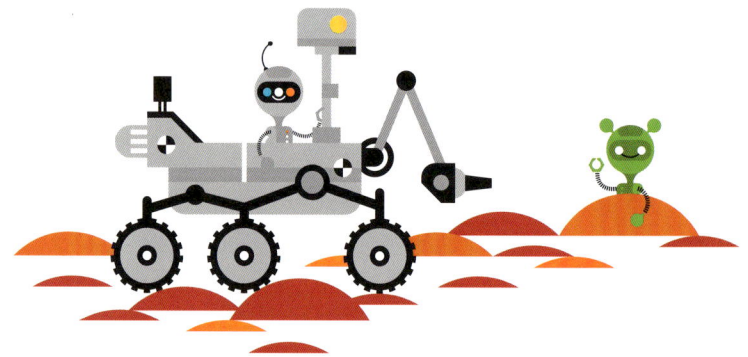
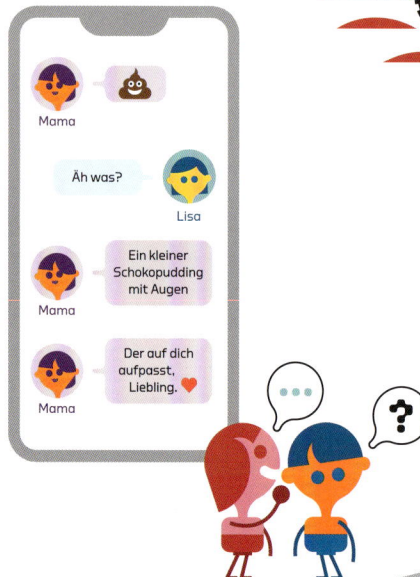

DURCHZÄHLEN !!

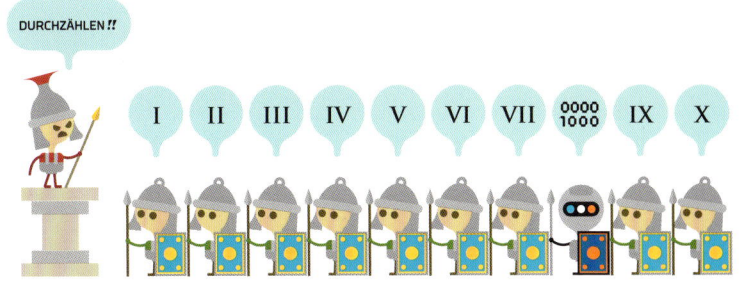

I II III IV V VI VII 0000 1000 IX X

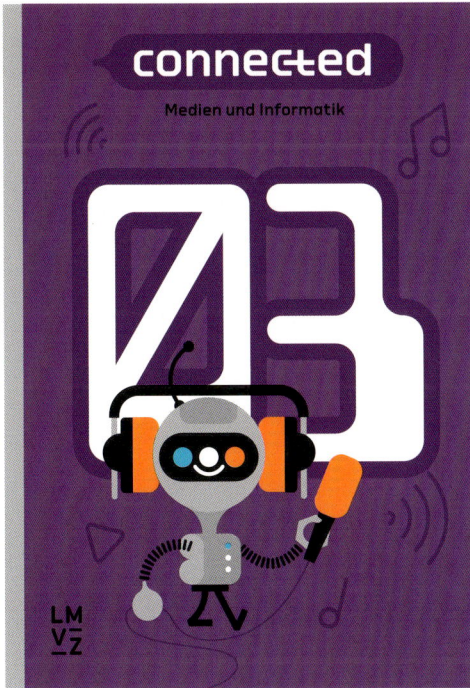

**Bot-E, Dron-E, Do-G,
BigBot & Care-B**
Character design,
3D renderings

Thanks for the tutorials:
Christoph Jenni & Twistereli

2019

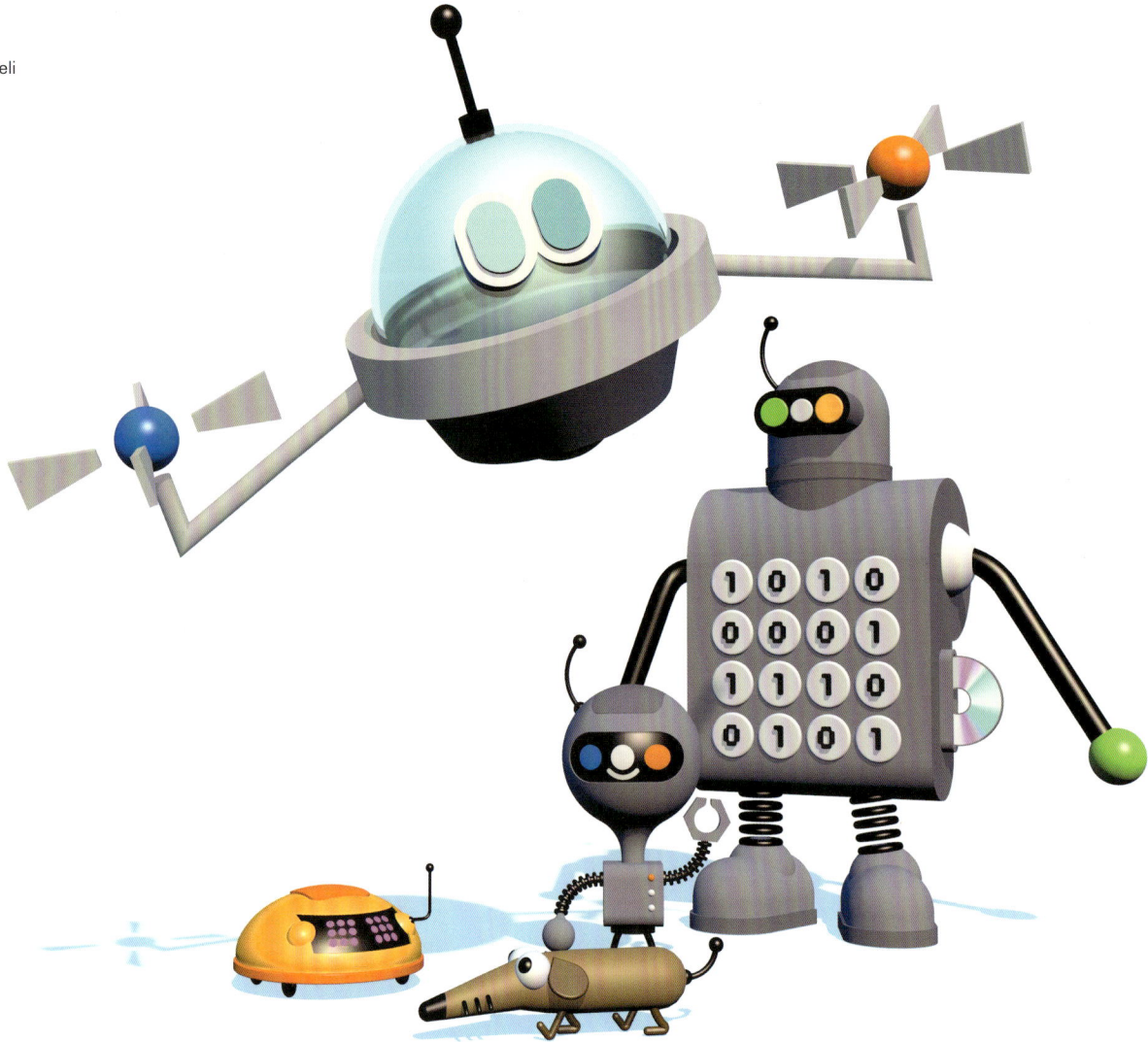

Connected 1–4
Book spreads chapter opening
illustrations of textbooks
for schoolkids learning and
understanding media and
informatics.

Client:
LMVZ Lehrmittelverlag Zürich

2017–2020

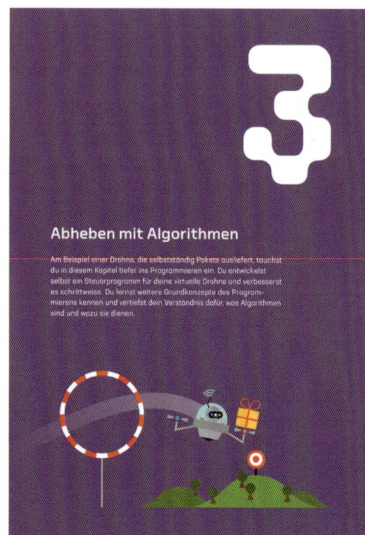

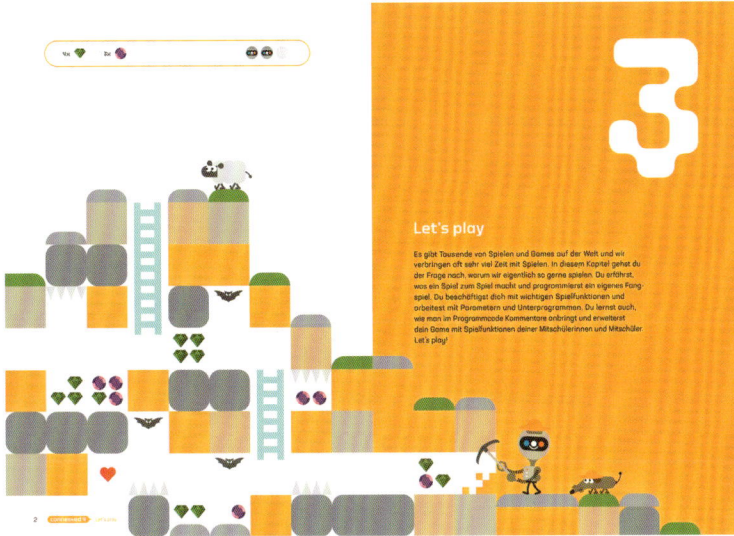

3

Let's play

Es gibt Tausende von Spielen und Games auf der Welt und wir verbringen oft sehr viel Zeit mit Spielen. In diesem Kapitel gehst du der Frage nach, warum wir eigentlich so gerne spielen. Du erfährst, was ein Spiel zum Spiel macht und programmierst ein eigenes Fang-spiel. Du beschäftigst dich mit wichtigen Spielfunktionen und arbeitest mit Parametern und Unterprogrammen. Du lernst auch, wie man im Programmcode Kommentare anbringt und erweiterst dein Game mit Spielfunktionen deiner Mitschülerinnen und Mitschüler. Let's play!

Bot-E V1.3.

5

Bilder: Punkt für Punkt

In diesem Kapitel erfährst du, wie der Computer Bilder speichert und worum sich digitale Bilder einfach bearbeiten lassen. Mit der Hilfe eines Malroboters lernst du, wie man eigene Bilder programmieren kann. Am Schluss weisst du auch, dass man Bildern nicht immer trauen kann.

2

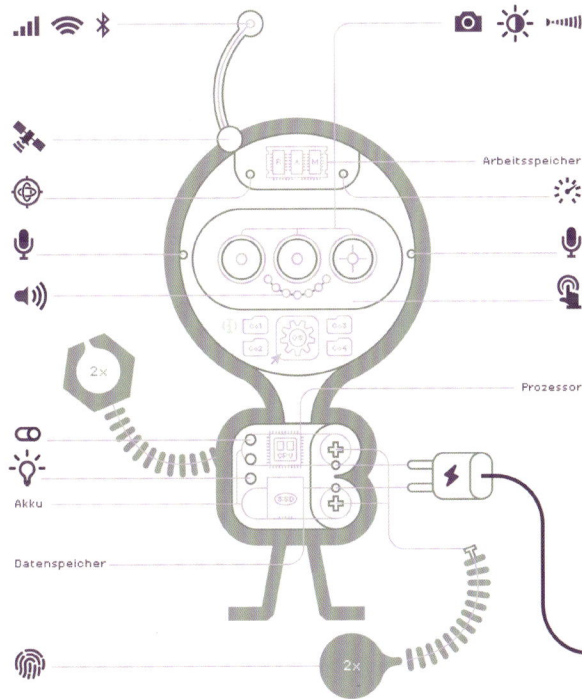

Digitale Geräte im Alltag

Du lernst in diesem Kapitel, was digitale Geräte sind und welche Aufgaben sie erfüllen. Du beschäftigst dich mit vielseitigen Geräten und mit solchen, die nur für einen ganz bestimmten Zweck eingesetzt werden. Dein Smartphone lernst du von einer neuen Seite kennen und du findest heraus, welche Daten die eingebauten Sensoren erfassen. Am Ende des Kapitels lernst du, wie Geräte im Smart Home vernetzt werden.

Arbeitsspeicher

Prozessor

Akku

Datenspeicher

2×

2×

BD Kickrom Mono
Typedifferent font

2016

www.typedifferent.com

BD KICKROM MONO

ABCDDEFFGG
HHIJJKKLMO
NNOOPQRSIT
UUVDVKYYZ
0123456789

[_T#%+'(+),.-./:;'\:="'?*■]
àöüÿàçtÿ¢$£¡¡ƒ฿£
«áâãäéèêëìíïîñôöòûüûù»

[64

BD KICKROMMONO*

BD KICKROM MONO

ABCDDEFFGGHHIJJKKL
MONNOOPQRSITUUVDVKYYZ
0123456789
[_T#%+'(+),.-./:;'\:="'?*■]
àöüÿàçtÿ¢$£¡¡ƒ฿£
«áâãäéèêëìíïîñôöòûüûù»

TASCHEN
RECHNER

JUNO*FIRST

INSERT COIN

ETC* ÷IBM [C64]

#RGB ■¥€$

+2X฿ XVNC /OK?

WELL, CERTAINLY NO ONE COULD HAVE BEEN
UNAWARE OF THE VERY STRANGE STORIES
FLOATING AROUND BEFORE HE LEFT. RUMORS
ABOUT SOMETHING BEING DUG UP ON THE MOON.
I NEVER GAVE THESE STORIES MUCH CREDENCE,
BUT PARTICULARLY IN VIEW OF SOME OF OTHER
THINGS THAT HAVE HAPPENED, I FIND THEM
DIFFICULT TO PUT OUT OF MY MIND. FOR
INSTANCE, THE DAY ALL OUR PREPARATIONS
WERE KEPT UNDER SUCH TIGHT SECURITY.

BEAMRIDER

PRESS START

Calcopac
Calculator app for iOS

2010–2016

Discontinued

App Store description:

Play your results as a little melody.

CALCOPAC is a "BEEP" more than a simple calculator for your iPhone & iPod Touch. It's a tribute to the legendary 8-Bit Videopac Game Computers released between 1978 and 1983.

CALCOPAC provides a stylish retro calculator with 2 skins and 24 8-Bit sound effects.

Features:
– Full operational calculator
– 2 skins / 24 sound effects
– Play result melody
– Sound On / Off / DEL key
– Copy / Paste
– Shake Ghost

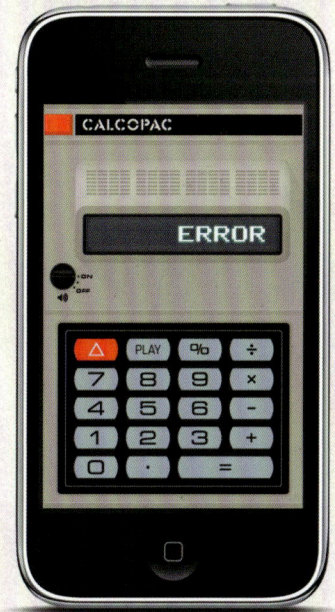

Change skin on backside

A little
BEEP
more than
a Calculator

$ 0.99

CALCOPAC

CALCOPAC for your iPhone & iPod Touch is a tribute to the legendary 8-Bit Videopac Game Computers released between 1978 and 1983.

CALCOPAC provides a stylish retro calculator with 2 skins and 24 8-Bit sound effects. By pressing down the Play key, it plays a little melody.

Play your results as a little melody

FEATURES*
• Full operational calculator
• 2 skins / 24 sound effects
• Play result melody
• Sound on/off / DEL key
• Shake Ghost

* Version 1.0 © 2010 Büro Destruct, Code: Bataais, Sound: Balduin, Graphics: Lopetz. Support & Feedback: calcopac@burodestruct.net

Some reviews:
For Odyssey² Fans! 8-bit heaven.
8-bit fans rejoice! If you ever had a Magnavox Odyssey², this will bring a smile to your face. The silver mode perfectly replicates the membrane keyboard, fonts, and sounds of the old videogame system. I only wish the buttons were larger because as a calculator, they are rather small. (I think the name refers to Videopac (?) which I believe is the name for the system in Europe). Here's hoping for more sounds and The Voice speech synthesis module! – navstar.

Calculation = fun
Adds character to an otherwise boring task. – Eatafat1.

I can't believe I paid for a calculator!!! But it's so worth it at only a buck! Very cool ... – joe m.

SIDE A

1. Galactic Gospel	4:57
2. Tall White	5:59
3. Massive Blackhole	7:06

SIDE B

1. Sentient Beings	5:57
2. Bewitched Scheme	7:16
3. Dark Matter	7:49

Qoniak:
Lionel Friedli, drums
Vincent Membrez, keys

Guests:
Joy Frempong, vocals
Flo Stoffner, guitar

All compositions by Qoniak
Recorded, mixed and mastered by Julien Fehlmann, Studio Mécanique, La Chaux-de-Fonds
Edited by Vincent Membrez

Qoniak thanks:
Joy, Flo, Jules, Matu & Everestrecords, Aline, Estelle, Ville de Bienne, Kanton Bern,
Pour-cent culturel Migros & Master Yoda.

SUISA®

www.qoniakmusic.ch
www.everestrecords.ch
℗&© 2013 by Qoniak and Everestrecords

Cover-Design by H1reber
www.burodestruct.net

er_lp_052

LC 23534

qoniak

ER
everestrecords

Qoniak –
Sentinent Beings
LP sleeve artwork

Client:
Qoniak

Published by Everest Records

2013

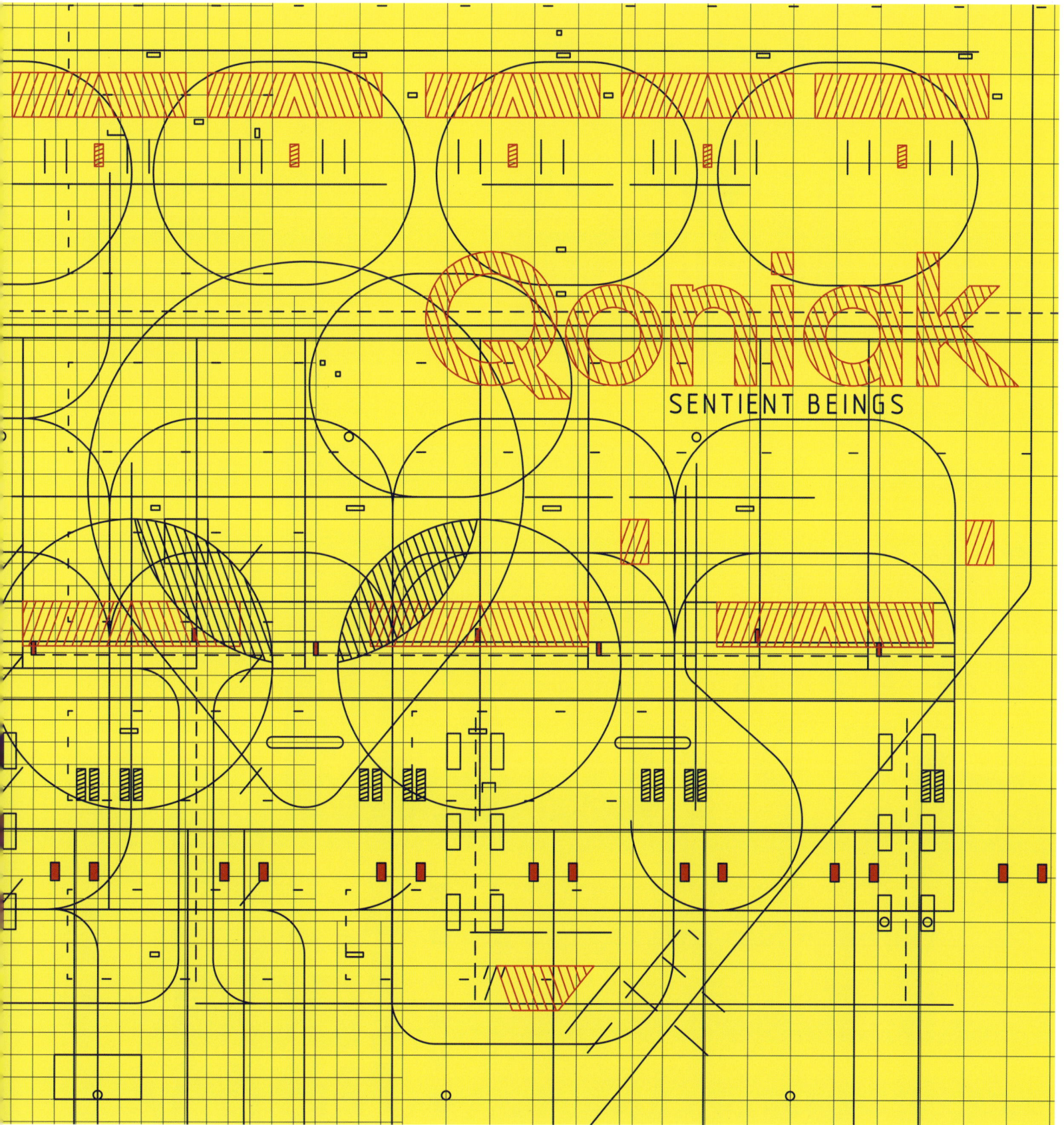

Qonick

SENTIENT BEINGS

Filewile & 340MIL
Clubnight poster and flyer
420 × 420 mm
120 × 120 mm

Client:
Dachstock, Reitschule Bern

2010

Flohmarkt
Fleamarket flyer
120 × 120 mm

Client:
Kitchener, Bern

2018

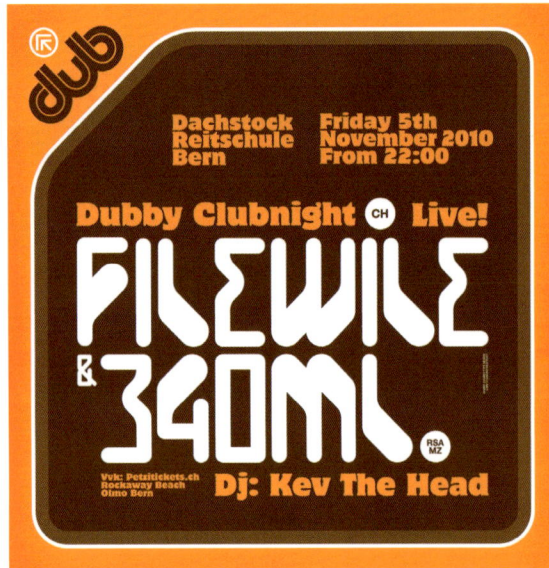

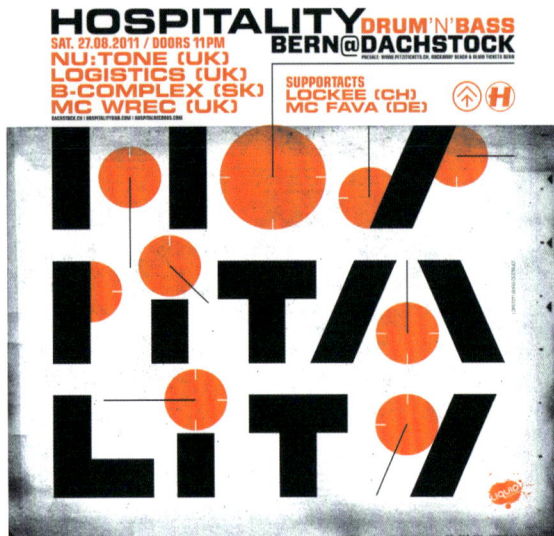

Hospitality
Labelnight poster and flyer
420 × 420 mm
120 × 120 mm

Client:
Dachstock, Reitschule Bern

2011

Balduin – Post from Mars
Digital album sleeve

Client:
Balduin

2014

Digital Playground
Festival poster and flyer
420 × 420 mm
120 × 120 mm

Client:
Dampfzentrale & Schlachthaus
Theater Bern

2011

LodelFizler
Digital clubnight flyer

Client:
auawirleben Theaterfestival,
Bern

2019

READABILITY IS THE UNDERWEAR
ORIGINALITY IS THE DRESS CODE

Bureau de Struct
hard 2 read – easy 2 remember

Side A

1. ASW   1:35
2. Busy penguin   2:55
3. Single manic episode   3:24
4. Hyper spectrum analysis   4:22
5. Foregone conclusion   2:30

Side B

6. Slow dreamer   2:45
7. High diving polarbear   4:03
8. Mood stabilizer   2:27
9. War 1.2   2:34
10. Shut up and sleep   1:33

www.everestrecords.ch • er_lp_037 • (C) & (P) 2010 by Meienberg

Supported by:
Amt für Kultur Kanton Bern, Burgergemeinde Bern,
KulturStadt Bern and Migros Kulturprozent.

Cover-Design by H1reber: büro destruct.10

7 640136 110209

MEIENBERG
RAPID CYCLING

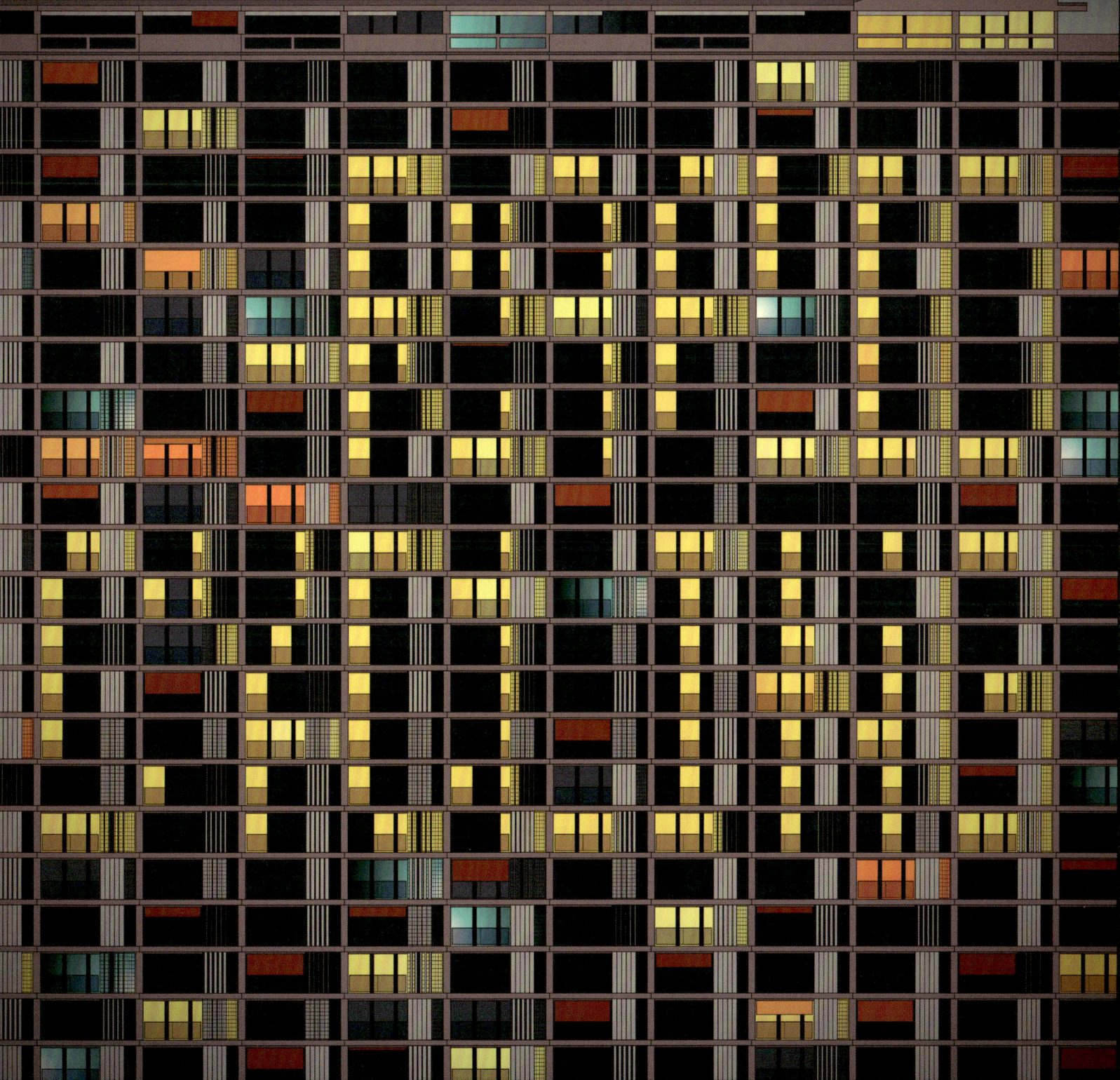

Meienberg – Rapid Cycling
LP sleeve artwork   Client: Meienberg

Top:
Stage sketch

2018

Middle and bottom:
Mich Gerber Monogram
and sketches for the album
Shoreline.

2018

Right page:
Mich Gerber – Shoreline
LP, CD sleeve artwork
and promotion poster.

Published by Irascible Music

Client:
Mich Gerber

2018

MICH GERBER   SHORELINE

BD:153

Tear-down art 1
San Theodoro, Sardinia, Italy

2015

It may be a sticker on a lamppost, an advertisement poster on the walkway, a reused shipping box waiting to be collected by the litter service. All of them may be attacked by unintended artists like the sun, rain or other vandals bleaching out, ripping off, scratching or altering the surface of their designed and printed victims.

What remains sometimes accidentally reminds me of visually striking abstract paintings. Their artists remain forever anonymous and that piece of art enjoys a short lifespan – unless it is recognized by someone that shares an eye for something that is commonly perceived as rubbish.

Lopetz, 2019

Tear-down art 2
Weingartstrasse,
Breitenrain, Switzerland

2019

Balduin – All in a Dream
LP sleeve artwork

Published by Sun Stone
Records, Chester, UK

Client:
Sun Stone Records,
Balduin

2014

www.balduin.org

SUNSTONE

This album is dedicated to my Fath[er]

Side One

1. Love Is You (3:06)
2. Which Dreamed It (2:02) *
3. Autumn (2:11)
4. Kite Come Back (3:21)
5. Glamour Forest (1:30)
6. Prisma Colora (3:05)
7. You Can Never Pipe My Fancy From My Dear (2:37) **
8. Father (3:40)

Sid[e]

1.
2.
3.
4.
5.
6.
7.
8.

SSLP1001

balduin

Songs written & recorded by Balduin at Creative Cookery Studio Bern, Switzerland, 2014.
* Music written by Sam Hutt (Boeing Duveen And The Beautiful Soup), 1968.
* Poem written by Lewis Carroll (1832-1898) from »Through the Looking-Glass, and
  What Alice Found There«, 1872.
** Lyrics »The Piper« by Robert Louis Stevenson (1850-1894).

Instruments:
Electric & acoustic guitars, bass, mellotron, electric & acoustic harpsichords,
piano, organ, vibraphone, lyre, sitar, tanpura, harmonium, wurlitzer, drums, tingsha,
tabla & percussion.

Premastered with a little help from Jan Stehle at Studio Mamma.
Vinyl mastering by Danny Woodward at Whitewood Studios.
Photos by Jun & Balduin. Collage by Balduin.
Sleeve designed in Büro Destruct by Lopetz & Balduin, Bern.

Sunstone Records | sunstonerecords.co.uk
℗ & © Balduin & Creative Cookery 2014 | balduin.org
Distributed by Clear Spot | clearspot.nl

(4:23)
(2:35)

STEREO
CAN ALSO BE PLAYED IN MONO

BD:157

デストラクト

ビュロ

BD

RAD
Homage to Marcel Duchamp's
"Bicycle Wheel" 1913.

2009

**The grass is always greener
on the other side**

Client:
auawirleben Theaterfestival,
Bern

Unpublished

2015

IN THE
RIGHT TIME
AT THE WRONG PLACE
IN THE WRONG TIME
AT THE
RIGHT PLACE

Bureau de Struct
optimiste sophistiqué

Constructivist
Artist pack for "Granimator"
iPad app

Client:
ustwo, UK

2010

Discontinued

Granimator™

Granimator by digital design studio ustwo™ is a sound based wallpaper creator that offers users a fully immersive touch and sound experience. The Granimator App for iPad offers an exquisite collection of ustwo designed packs which gives users access to a large choice of graphical elements (styles, shapes and backgrounds) which they can tap, pinch and drag across the screen to create stunning compositions and soundscapes.

Users can download more packs from world-renowned designers: Airside, Pete Fowler, Büro Destruct, James Joyce, Rexbox and Moving Brands. This is an iPad app designed to enable users to create something beautiful, while being fully engaged with the creative process.

Mills, co-founder of ustwo

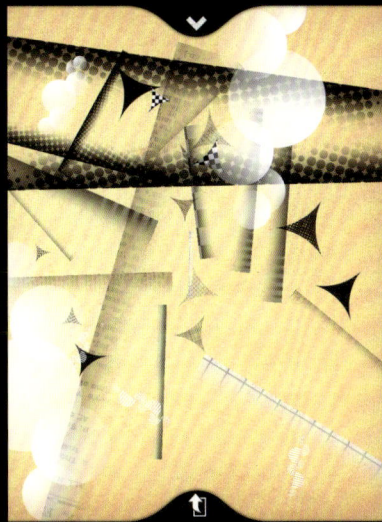

Become a constructivist with the artist pack of swiss based graphic design studio Büro Destruct. Symbols, styles and backgrounds are inspired by Russian Constructivism, German Dadaism, Bauhaus and the work of early Swiss graphic designers. All carefully crafted design parts are flavoured with typical Büro Destruct icons and Japanese Katakana characters from their Typedifferent typefaces.

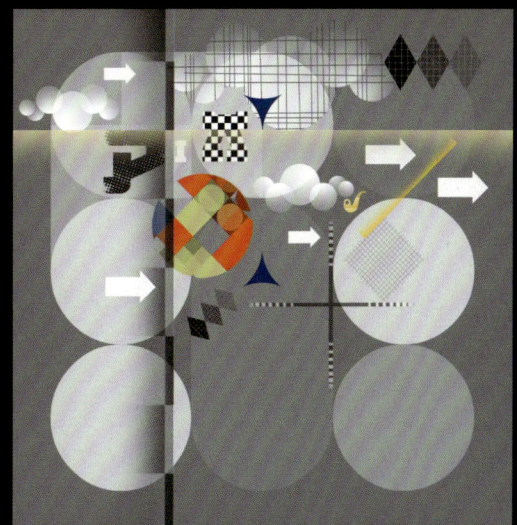

Radio Rabe
25 years anniversary poster
and "Unity in diversity" logos.

Client:
Radio Rabe, Bern

2020

Right page:
Zirkusschule Bern
Identity and various
printed materials for a
circus school.

Client:
Zirkusschule Bern

2017

100 Seconds of Knowledge
22 illustrations, each of them
drawn in under 100 seconds
for the "100×100 Sekunden
Wissen – Takeaway" book
written by author Thomas
Weibel.

Published by Schwabe Verlag
Basel, Switzerland

Client:
Thomas Weibel

2012

ISBN 978-3796528422

www.100-sekunden.ch
www.lopetz.com

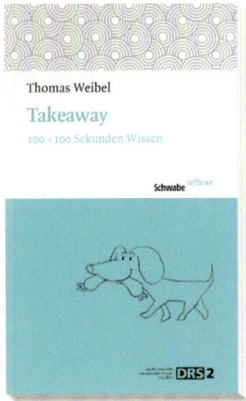

Post-it

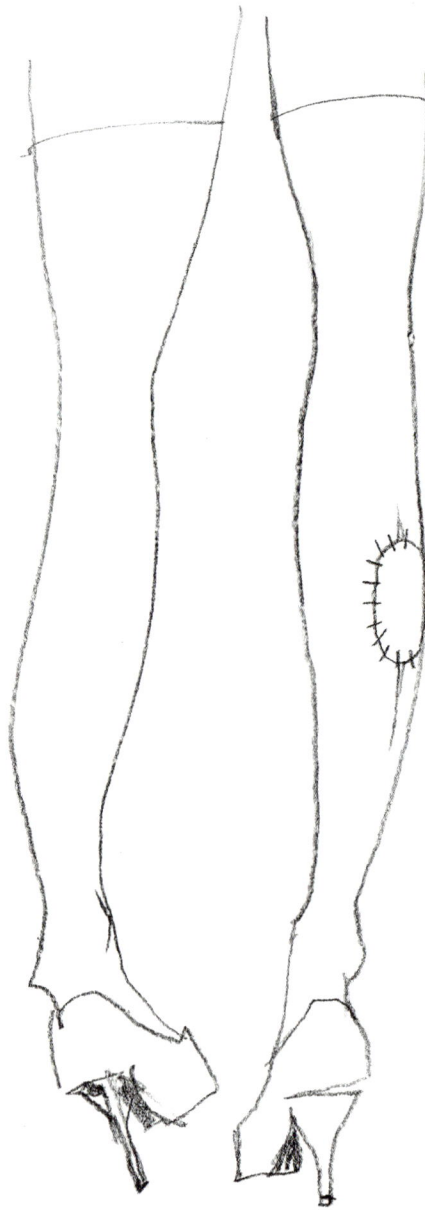

nylon

larry laffer

RR
t t
R t

atari

computermaus

harley davidson

wurmer

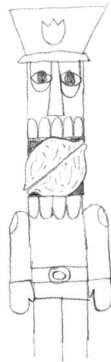

enigma

krawatte

walkman

BD:166

BD Aubergin
Variable Typedifferent font

One of six BD rub on font sheets. Limited Edition.
170 × 255 mm

2020

www.typedifferent.com
www.burodiscount.net

typedifferent.com «BD Aubergin» designed by Lopetz in 2020. © büro destruct 2020
Digitally available on www.typedifferent.com and www.mylonts.com print&proof rubon®
PRINTED IN GERMANY BD164

Boulevard

Pattern design consisting of more than 120 newspaper snippets for a Swatch special edition dedicated to the sixtieth anniversary of Blick – Switzerlands daily boulevard-newspaper.

Left page:
Proposals "Dada Bauhaus" and "Headline Punk"

Right page:
Final pattern

Client:
Blick, Ringier AG

2019

Leftovers composition

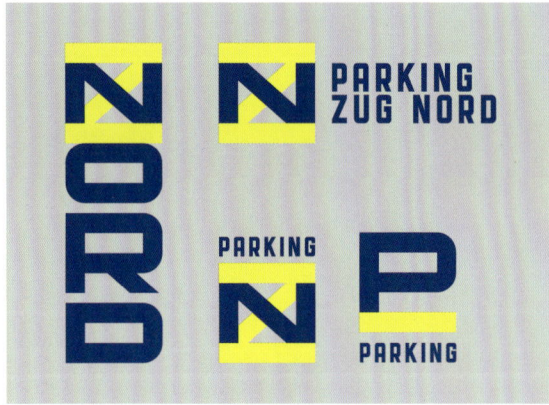

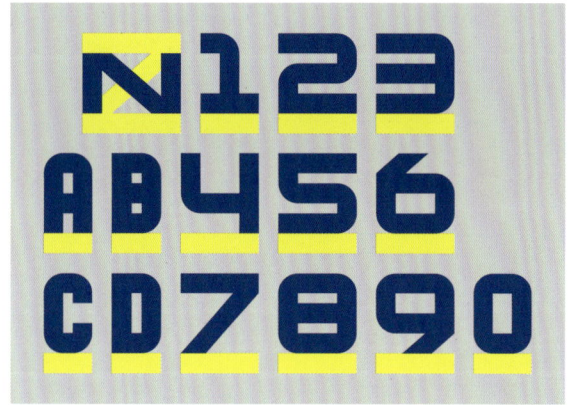

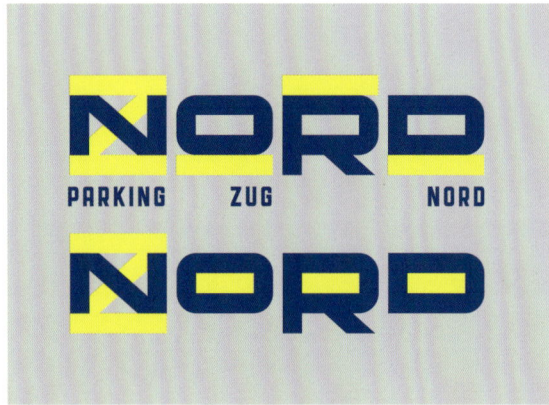

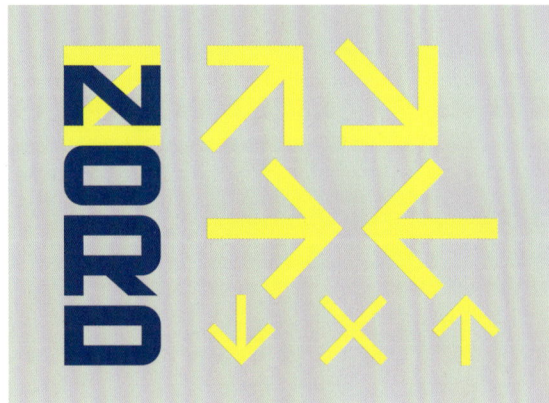

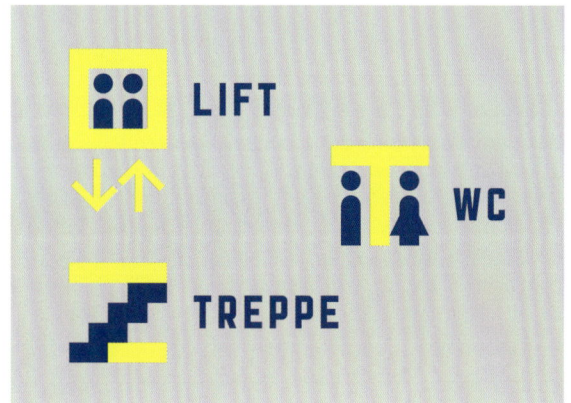

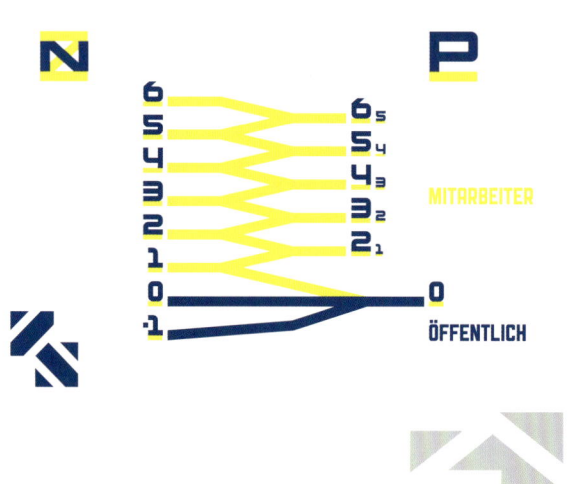

BD:170

Left page:
Z-Nord
Design proposal of logotype
and signage of a parking lot.

Client:
Hosoya Schaefer Architects,
Zurich

2019

Turnhalle Bitzius
Signage design for the school
sports hall "Turnhalle Bitzius".

Client:
wbarchitekten, Bern

Photos:
Architekturfotografie
Gempeler

2017

TURN HALLEN BITZIUS 15A

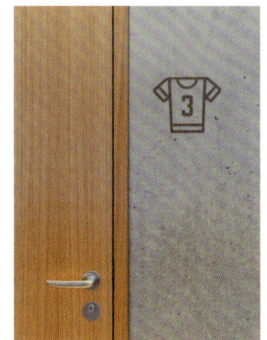

Swiss Coloring Book
Illustrations of 18 famous
Swiss people from the world
of art, architecture, literature,
sport, business and science.

The box contains 18 named
crayons produced by Swiss
based "Caran d'Ache" and the
coloring book published in a
total of six languages.

Client:
Federal Department
of Foreign Affairs FDFA,
Presence Switzerland

2015

Featured Swiss personalities:

Wilhelm Tell, Helvetia, Leonhard Euler, Jean-Jacques Rousseau, Alfred Escher, Johanna Spyri, Henry Dunant, Albert Einstein, Auguste Piccard, Le Corbusier, Sophie Taeuber-Arp, Alberto Giacometti, Friedrich Dürrenmatt, Jean Tinguely, Ursula Andress, Mario Botta, Simon Ammann, Roger Federer

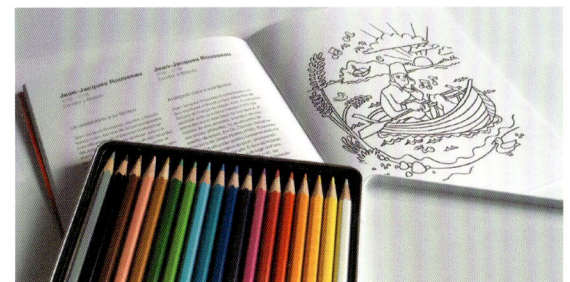

SEVEN

Air to Ground A-Seven
Snowboard jacket design
collaboration.

Art direction:
Toshio Kondo & Akihiro
Ikegoshi

Client:
A-Seven Osaka Japan,
Descente Ltd. Osaka Japan

Photos: OKA-Z

2013

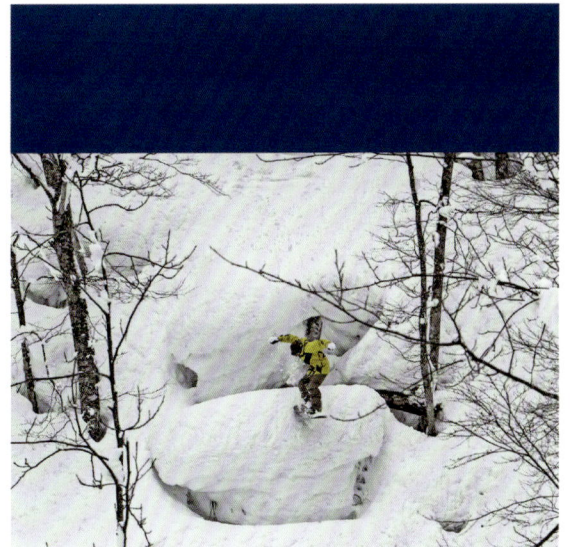

blablabla …
Monthly programme
posters
895×1280 mm

Client:
Kulturhallen
Dampfzentrale
Bern

2001

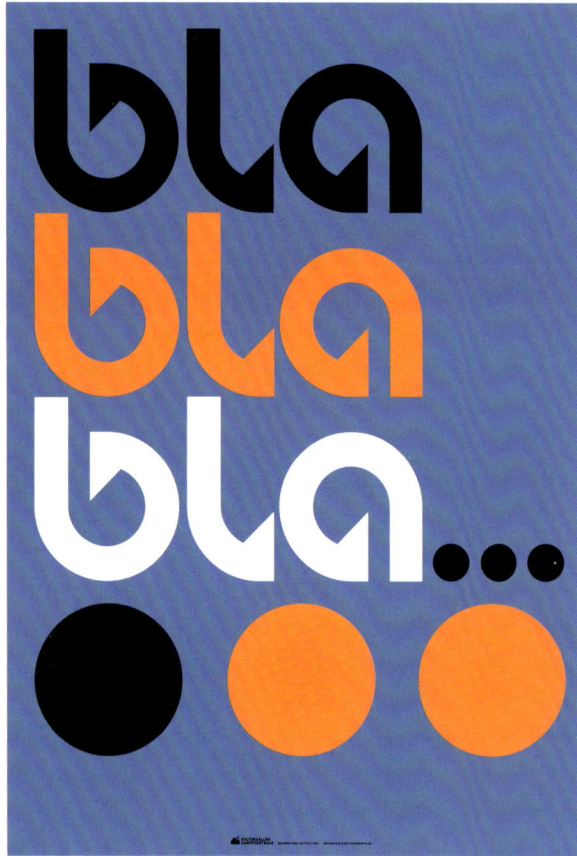

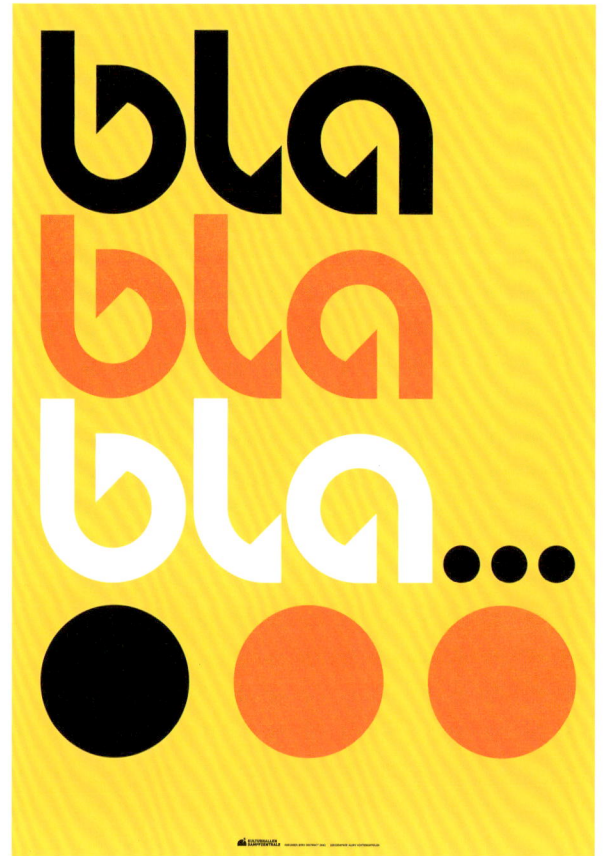

**Mute-ation of
Communication**
BD Corona Talk
Youtube video

Lockdown –
Spring 2020

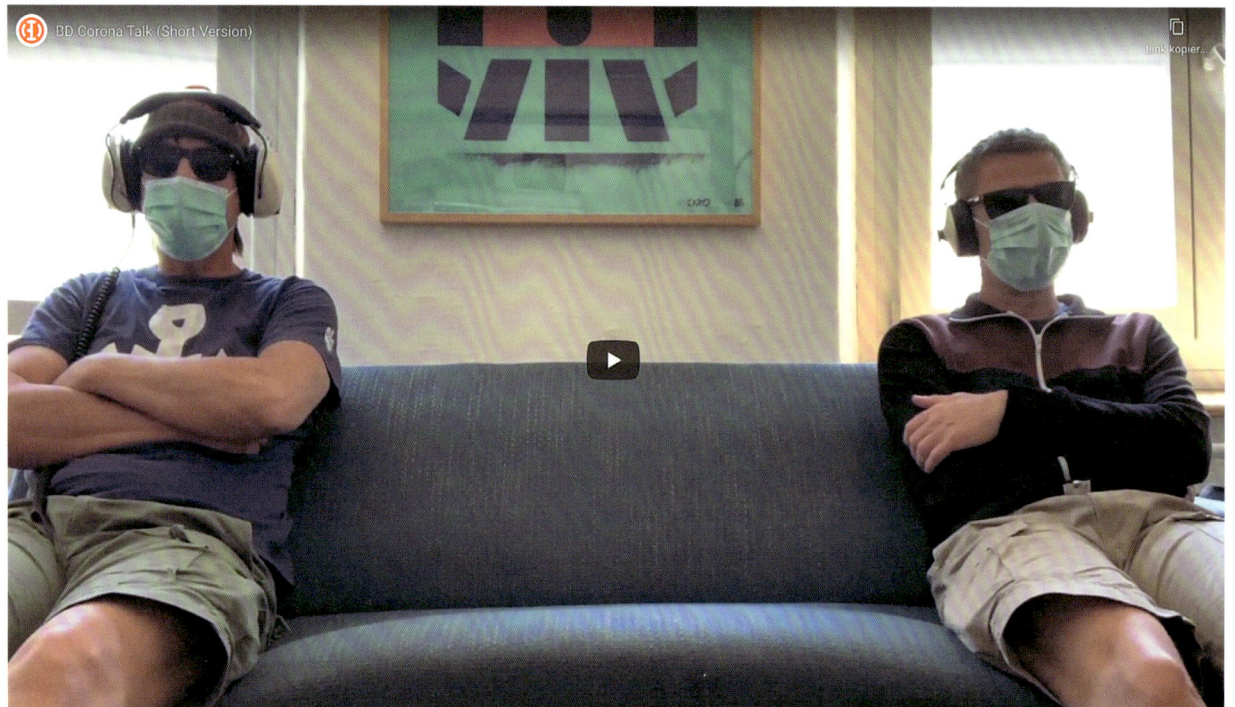

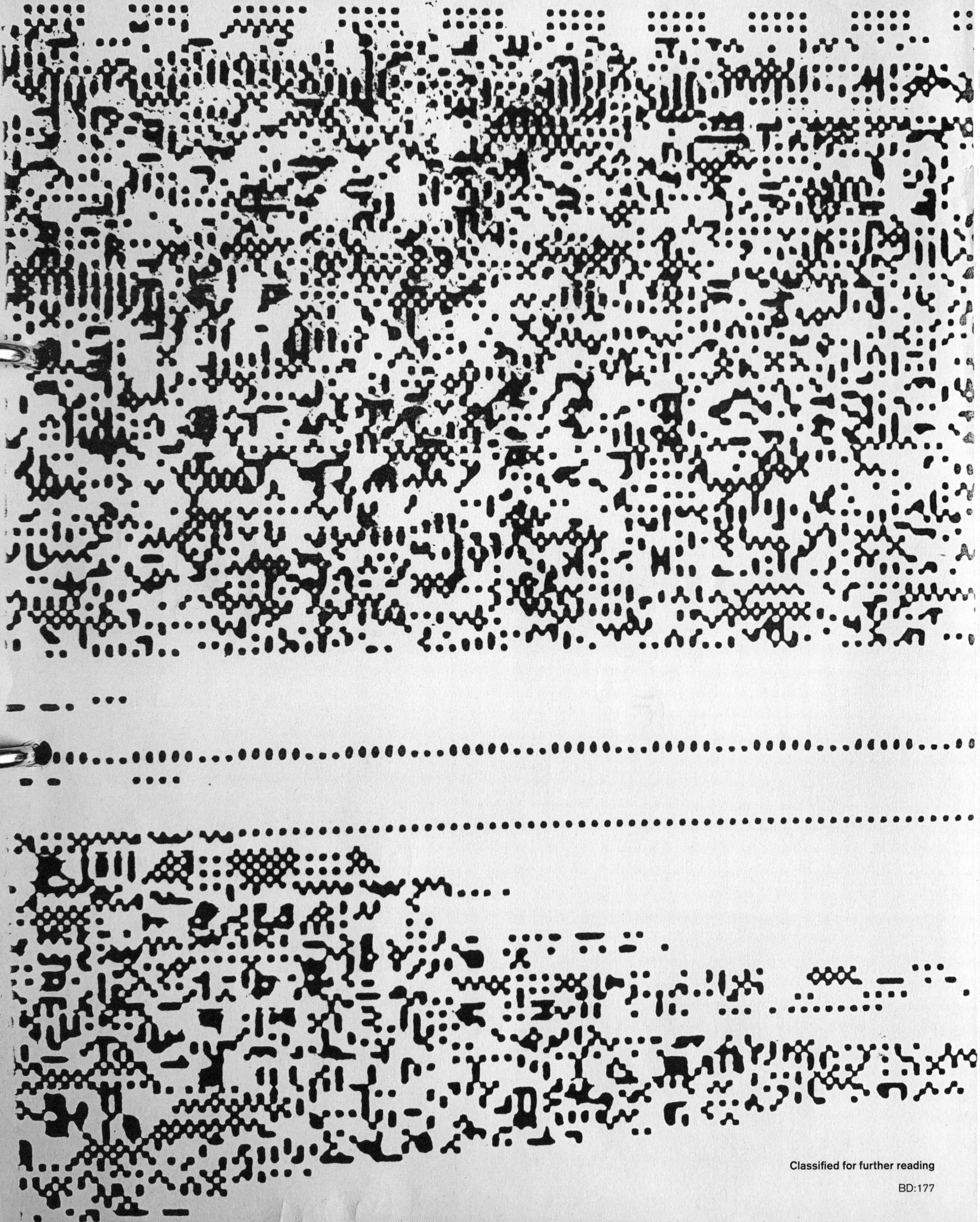

Classified for further reading

Seaworld
Drawing by Nara Nino
(son of Lopetz at the age
of 9).

2015

Naranino Font
by Nara Nino
(at the age of 6).

2012

www.typedifferent.com

Font royalties for Nara's
piggybank

CHILDLIKE
LIGHTHEARTEDNESS
IS ART

Bureau de Struct

gravité zéro

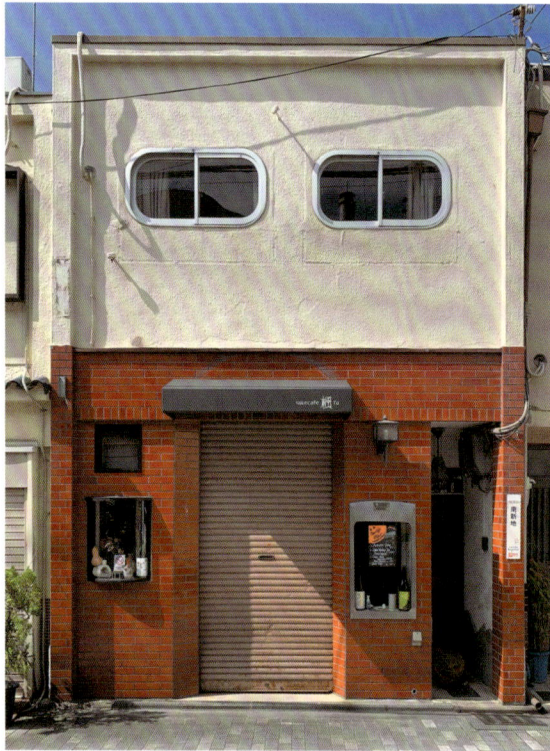

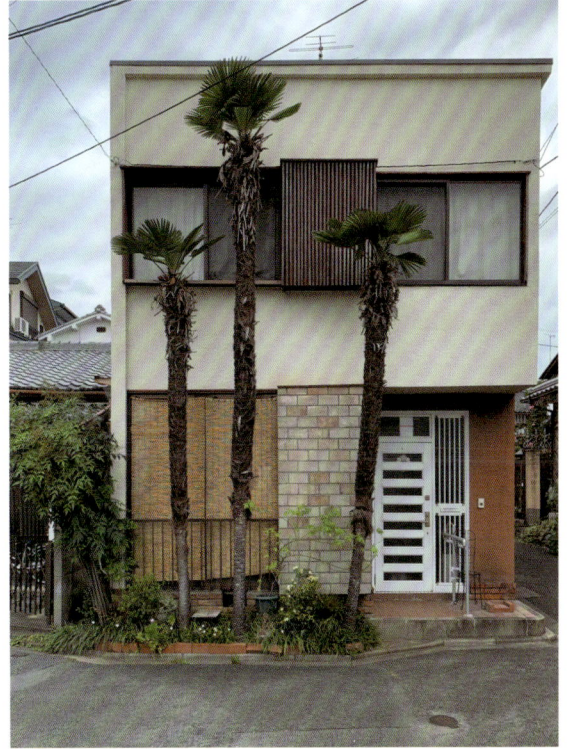

Face Off! – A black comedy with a white smile
Theater poster

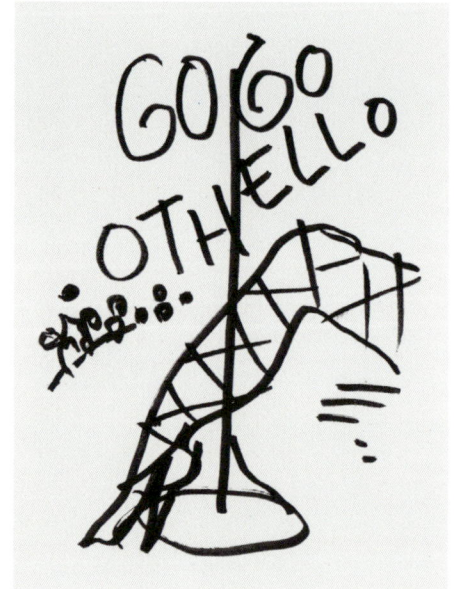

Top left:
Face Off! – A black comedy with a white smile
Theater poster
420×594mm

2015

Bottom left:
Black Off! – A white comedy with a black smile
Theater poster
420×594mm

2016

GoGo Othello – Standup Bourlesque Soul Stripping
Theater poster, sketch and draft.
895×1280mm
420×594mm

Client:
Manaka Empowerment Prod., Schlachthaus Theater Bern

2020

Performer Ntando Cele uniquely blurs the boundaries between physical theater, video installation, stand-up comedy and performance. Her approach is often that she creates many different stereotypes using humour, charm and exuberance in order to question and fight them. With this method, she explores black and white identity, racism and prejudice from different perspectives.

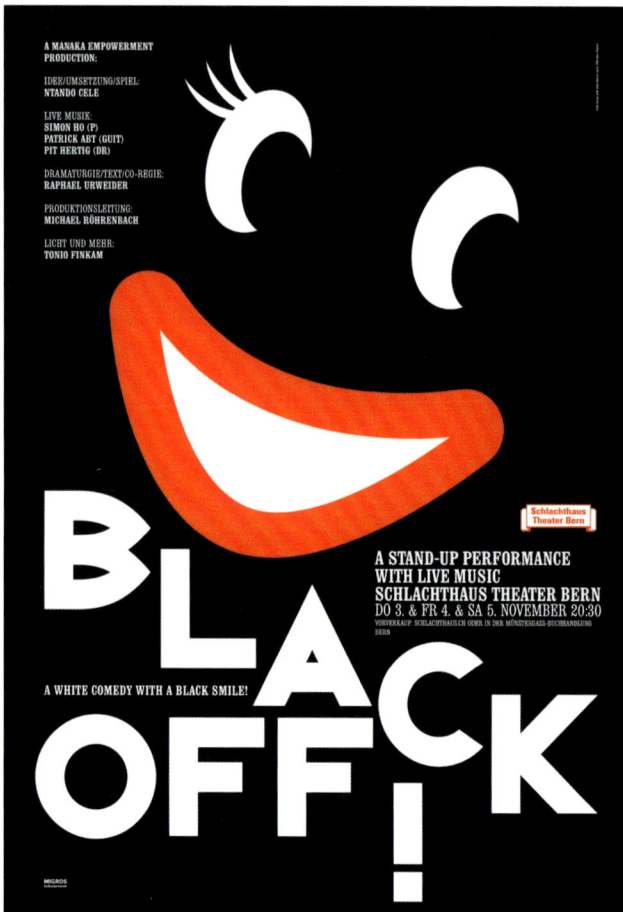

Black Off! – A white comedy with a black smile
Theater poster

GoGo Othello – Standup Bourlesque Soul Stripping
Theater poster

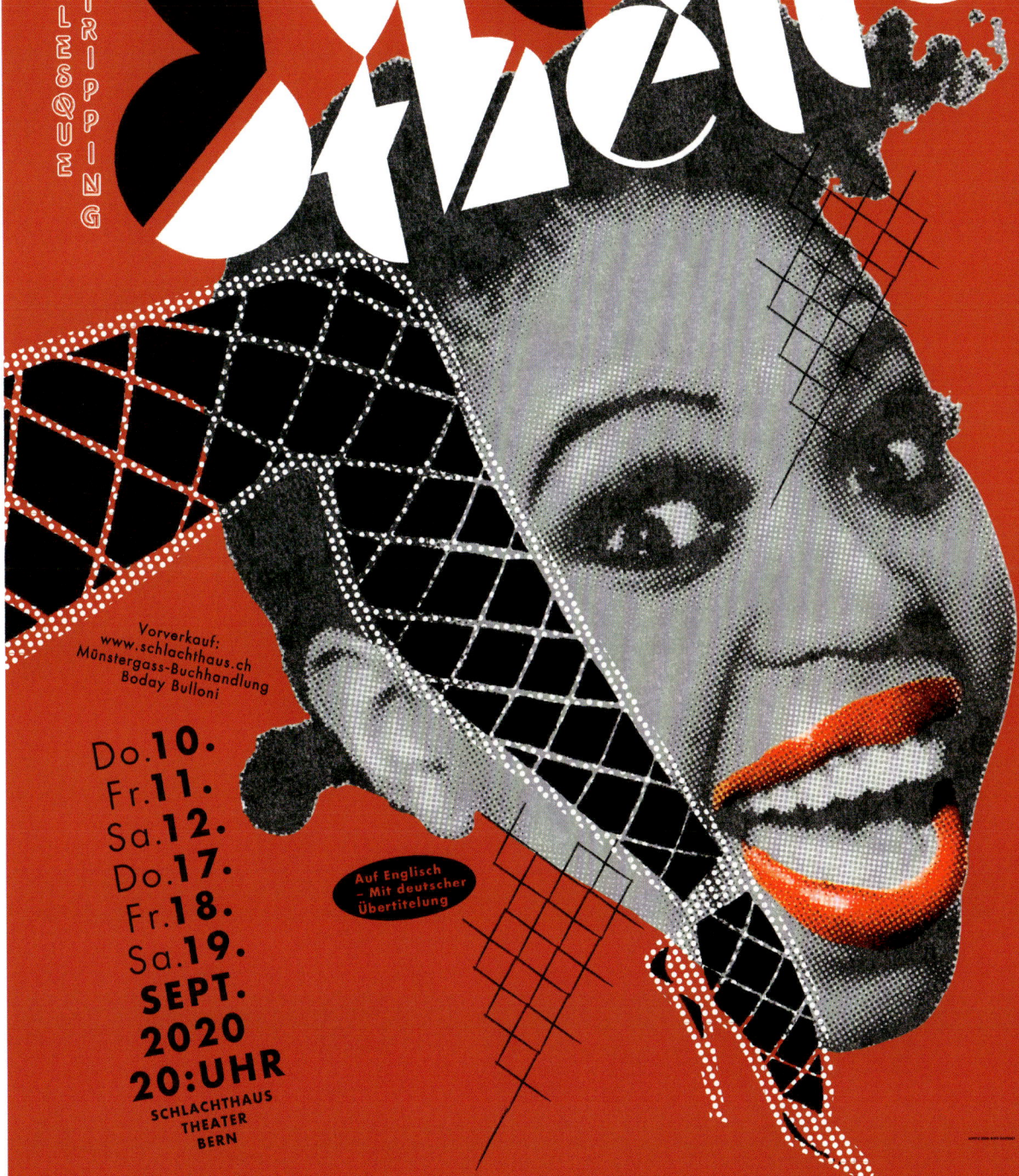

BD:183

Wertschöpfungskette

Gütesiegel

Transformation

Pendlergeschichten
25 illustrations for the book
"dazwischen" created during
the first Corona lockdown.

The book contains 24 short
stories about commuting.

ISBN 978-3-033-07961-8

Client:
Mark Balsiger, Border Crossing

2020

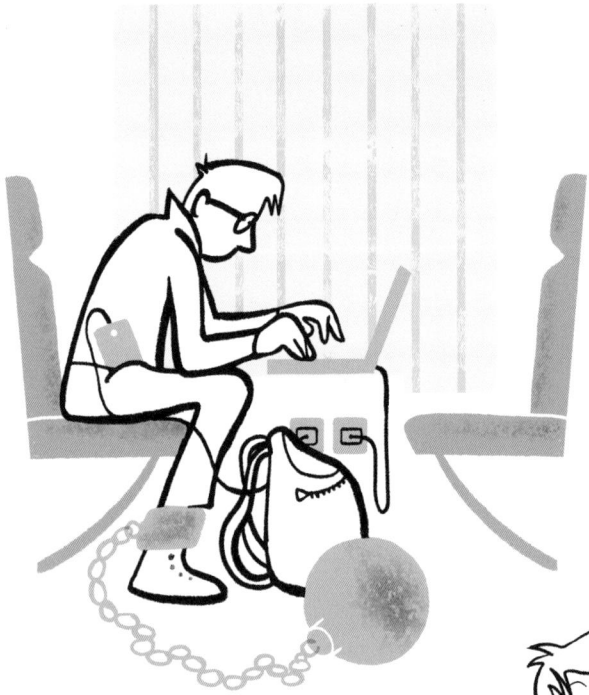

DANDOULA TALA

JMO – Dandoula Tala
CD sleeve artwork

Shapes by Lucy (daughter of
Marc "MB" Brunner at the age
of 14).

Client:
JMO, Jan Galega Brönnimann

2020

Right page:
**Grand Mother's Funk –
The Big Pie**
CD sleeve and digital release
singles artworks.

Client:
GMF, Grand Mother's Funk

2020

BATA
KUNOU
NITTÉ
HANG LOOSE
HANG EVER
NANAITA
BAËNG
ALI FRING AFRICA
NYONG
JOULO
TALA DYLA
BAYIKO MO FREE
TA

Dandoula Tala

Jan Galega Brönnimann
Moussa Cissokho
Omri Hason

JAN GALEGA BRÖNNIMANN
CONTRA ALTO- AND BASS CLARINET, SOPRANO SAXOPHONE,
MBIRA, KASS KASS
MOUSSA CISSOKHO
KORA, VOCAL, BOLON, TALKIN DRUM
OMRI HASON
PERCUSSION, HANG, KALIMBA, TONGUE DRUM
BOUBA CISSOKHO
NGONI ON TRACK 1

THANKS TO
LUDI, EVI, CISSOKHO FAMILY, ROB, CHRIGU, MARGU BÜRO DESTRUCT,
CHRISTIAN AND CPL MUSIC, ANDI

PHOTOGRAPHED
CHRISTA ENGSTLER
SLEEVE DESIGNED
AT BÜRO DESTRUCT
MARC BRUNNER
MIXED AND MASTERED
CHRISTOPH UTZINGER
AT THE ZOO, BERN
ROB AEBERHARD
SWITZERLAND
RECORDED 2019
BOUBA CISSOKHO
NGONI ON TRACK 1
OMRI HASON
PERCUSSION, HANG, KALIMBA,
TONGUE DRUM
MOUSSA CISSOKHO
KORA, VOCAL, BOLON,
TALKIN DRUM
JAN GALEGA BRÖNNIMANN
CONTRA ALTO- AND BASS CLARINET,
SOPRANO SAXOPHONE, MBIRA,
KASS KASS

JAN GALEGA BRÖNNIMANN
MOUSSA CISSOKHO
OMRI HASON

CPL042
℗+©2020
SUISA
LC23533

CPL042 LC23533
www.cpl-music.de
©+℗2020 by jmo & cpl music

4 251329 500283

contact: www.jangalegabroennimann.ch

Burgergemeinde Bern
Kultur Stadt Bern
SWISSLOS
Kultur Kanton Bern

BD:190

GRAND MOTHER'S FUNCK GMF

THE BIG
PiE

GMF

GRAND MOTHER'S FUNCK

WHO
IS WHO

LIV
REMIX
CLUB
VERS. GMF

GRAND MOTHER'S FUNCK

SPANISH
MOSS

GMF

GRAND MOTHER'S FUNCK

SPIRIT

GMF

GRAND MOTHER'S FUNCK

IT'S
PAYDAY
TEDDY

GMF

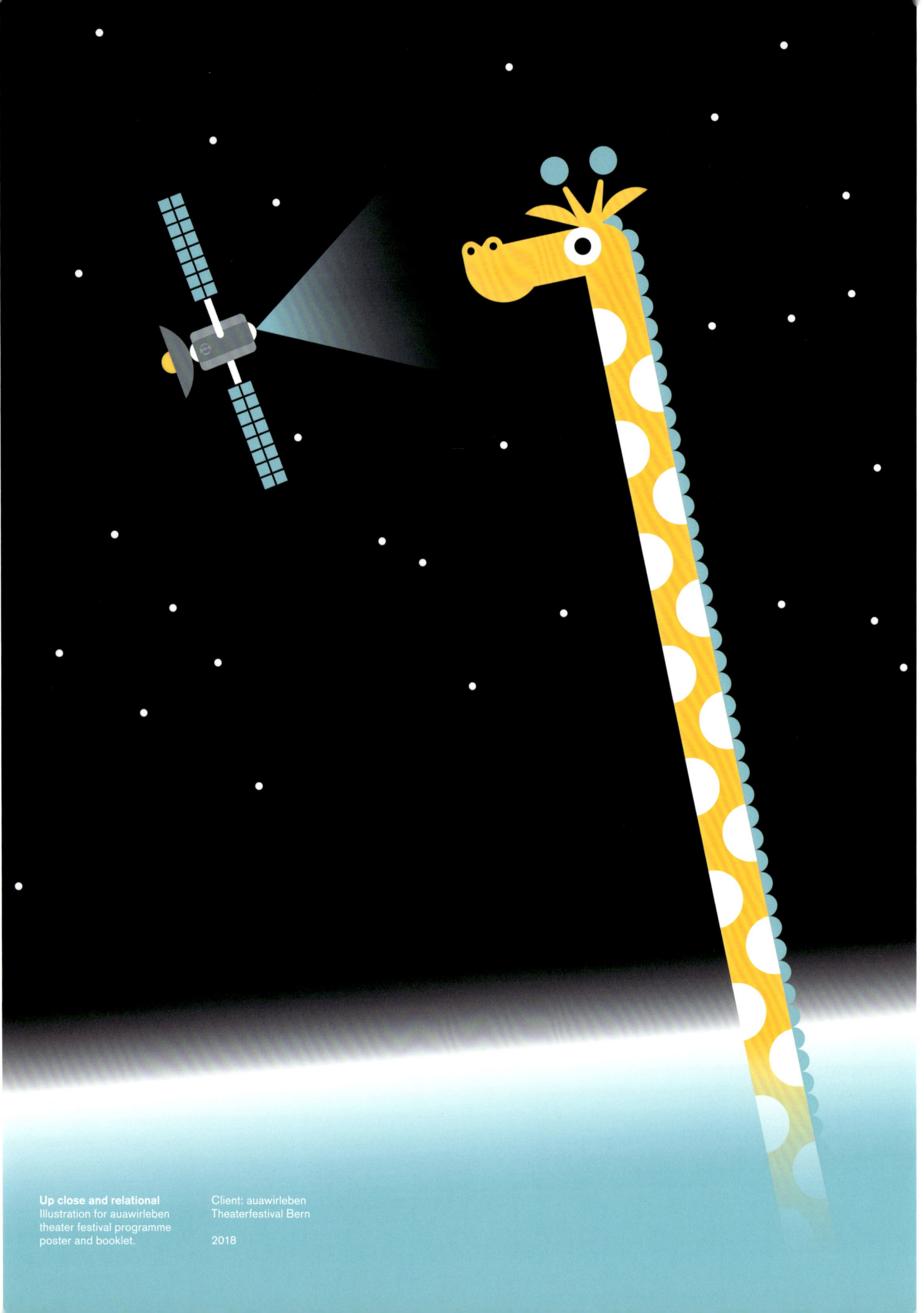

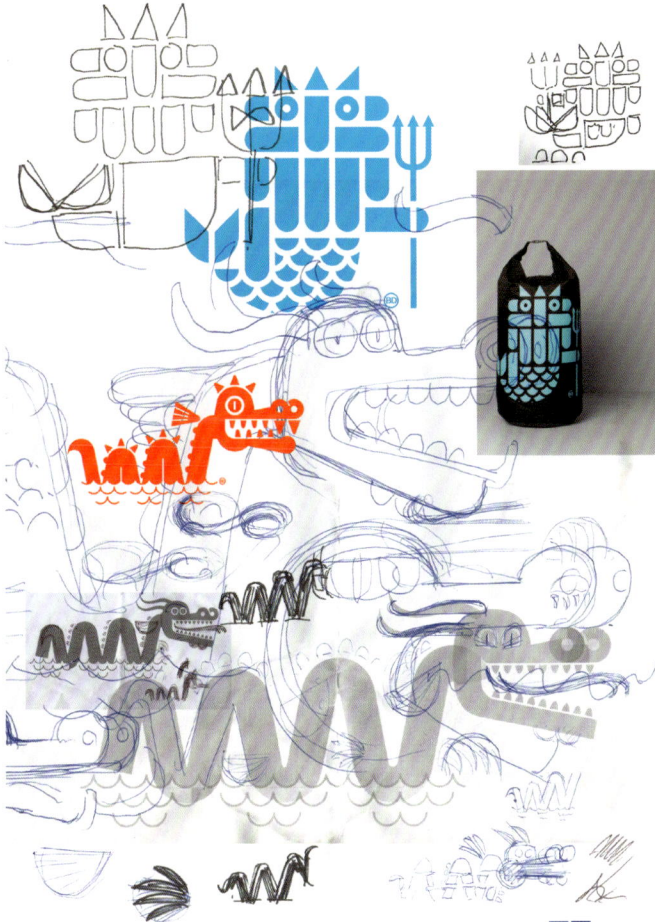

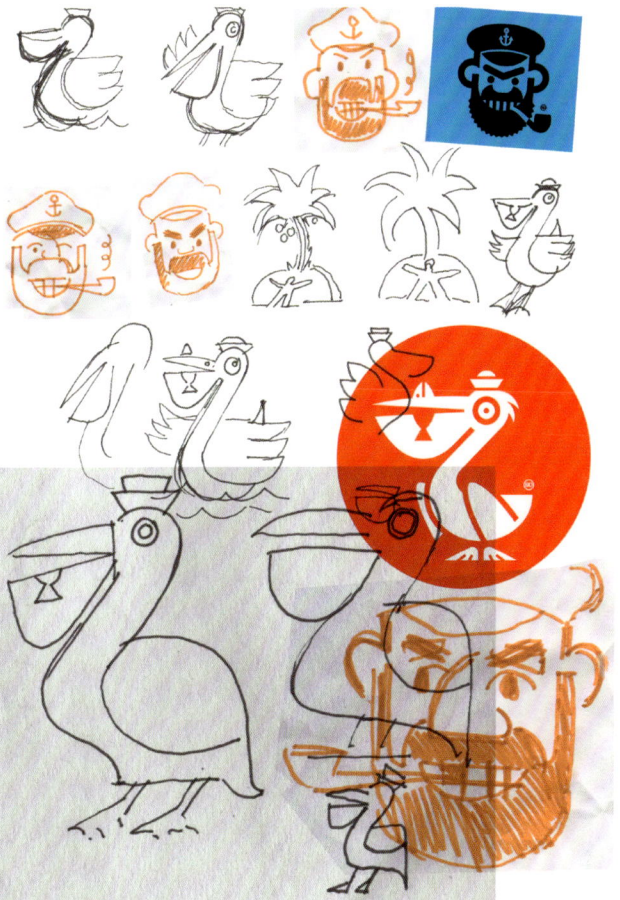

aarebag.ch

Previous page:
Aarebags
Character sketches

mAARE
Character designs
for Aarebag collection and
BD "mAARE" iPhone App.

2013–2020

www.aarebag.ch
www.maare.be

Aarebags
Drybag designs in co-production with Kitchener, Bern.
Since 2013 every summer
a new collection is released.

2013–2020

www.aarebag.ch

Top left to bottom right:
Captain (2017), Shark (2020), Koi (2018), Mermaid (2016),
Aarepirat (2014), Saba (2018), Walrus (2018), Pelican (2018),
Seagull (2015), Lobster (2017), Graphic Waves (2020), Ship (2014)

Top left to bottom right:
Seastars (2017), Whale (2013), Sun (2017), Fugu (2019),
Neptun (2016), Submarine (2014), Gardeneels (2019), Aarnie (2018),
Jellyfish (2016), Anchor (2013), Octopus (2015), Sea Medley (2019)

Garden Eels
Drybag pattern design
in co-production with
Kitchener, Bern.

2019

www.aarebag.ch

The garden eels are the subfamily Heterocongrinae in the conger eel family Congridae. The majority of garden eels live in the Indo-Pacific, but species are also found in warmer parts of the Atlantic Ocean (including the Caribbean) and East Pacific. These small eels live in burrows on the sea floor and get their name from their practice of poking their heads from their burrows while most of their bodies remain hidden. Since they tend to live in groups, the many eel heads "growing" from the sea floor resemble the plants in a garden.

They vary greatly in colour depending on the exact species involved. The largest species reaches about 120 cm in length, but most species do not surpass 60 cm.

Wikipedia

BD

Rimini
Illustration
and logotype

2020

Unpublished

könizer

Könizer
Logotype and icons for the
public pool "Könizer".

Client:
Gemeinde Köniz, Bern

2020

J'aime la mer
Logotype

2021

Terra Vecchia
Animals and vehicles
illustrations for sand-blasted
prints on drinking glasses.

Client:
Stiftung Terra Vecchia,
Glasart

2016–2020

Bottom
**Sauberes Wasser –
Bauern für Generationen**
Postcard
210×105 mm

Client:
Stiftung Terra Vecchia,
IP-Suisse

2019

BD:202

Lagerverkauf
Flyers
105 × 148 mm
210 × 148 mm

Client: Kitchener, Bern

2012

Dig'n'Doz
Logotype for a kids app concept
with diggers & dozers.

2013, Unrealized

This and previous spread:
Schauspielhaus Zürich
Art direction, collages and
editorial design of season
2016/17 book.

Photos of actors: Lieblinge

Cover photo: René Reichelt

Realisation:
SchmauderRohr

Client:
Schauspielhaus Zürich

2016

Schauspielhaus
Zürich
2016/17

Schiffbau/Box
Uraufführung am 11. September 2015

von Nolte Decar

Regie: Sebastian Kreyer
Bühne und Kostüme: Matthias Nebel

Koproduktion mit dem
Deutschen Theater Berlin

Der neue Himmel

Die ganze Welt scheint hier Krisengebiet, wenn Drohnenangriffe, seltsame Einschläge oder plötzlich niedergehende Geschosse das Leben dieser Figuren erschüttern: In Kolumbien kommen sich zwei Teenager näher, bevor eine Rakete ihren Schulbus trifft. In der Antarktis führen Xiao und Chester Vater-Sohn-Gespräche, als plötzlich ihre Forschungsstation in Flammen steht. Nur in Alaska ist nichts los oder vielleicht ist der Detonation am Ende doch nicht nur ein Böller in einem Briefkasten? Ob die Einschläge in einem Zusammenhang stehen, oder von einem zentralen Ort gesteuert werden? Im Westen, in der nordenglischen Stadt Whitby, scheint alles zusammenzukommen: ein Inspektor Nordt einen alten Fall aufrollt. Es war damals kein Unfall, ermittelt er, sondern eine Luft-Boden-Rakete. Und der Chauffeur kann es nicht gewesen sein! In den skurrilkomischen Szenen an den globalumspannenden Schauplätzen erleben wir Alltagsgeschichten, in denen uns die Figuren seltsam nah sind und uns dann jedes Mal grob entrissen werden, wenn die Erzählstränge unvermittelt abreissen.

Das Autorenduo Nolte Decar, Jahrgänge 1988 und 1987, entwirft ein weltweites kriminologisches Panorama aus Nahaufnahmen, durchsetzt von Elementen aus kriminalgeschichten und Film noir. „Der neue Himmel" von Jakob Nolte und Michel Decar zählt zu den Gewinnerstücken des Autorenwettbewerbs der Autorentheatertage am Deutschen Theater Berlin, wo die Zürcher

Inszenierung im Juni 2015 ihre Uraufführung erlebt, bevor sie im September in Zürich Premiere feiert.

Der Regisseur Sebastian Kreyer studierte Theaterwissenschaft, Philosophie und Soziologie. 2013 war er mit seiner Kölner Inszenierung „Die Glasmenagerie" von Tennessee Williams zum Festival Radikal Jung eingeladen, seither inszeniert er u. a. am Volkstheater München, am Theater Bremen und am Schauspielhaus Hamburg. Am Schauspielhaus Zürich inszenierte er bereits das Kurzdrama „Man bleibt, wo man hingehört und wer nicht bleiben kann, gehört hab nirgends hin" von Katja Brunner im Rahmen des Festivals „Transit Zürich".

Ein Liebhaberstück

(Arbeitstitel)
Pfauen
Uraufführung April 2016

von René Pollesch

Regie: René Pollesch
Bühne: Bert Neumann

„Wir haben eine Fähigkeit, die unsere eigentliche Potenz ist, und zwar, in jedem, den wir begegnen, und der nur Töne von sich gibt, tendenziell die irgendeine wie ein inneres Leben zu vermuten. Das können wir bei jedem toten Gegenstand. Wir geben jedem Beispiel unserer Liebe. Ich halt das jahrelang gemacht, weisst du. Und jetzt stellst du vor mir, und mir gelingt das plötzlich nicht mehr. Ich erlebe also, wie das reisst. Und weil es mir an dir nicht gelingt, kann ich mich selber auch nicht aufhalten. Und das ist das ganze Geheimnis, ich kann das nicht mehr, an der irgendwas herzustellen, eine Subjektivität, die mich aufhält. Unsere Liebesgeschichte hat sehr viel mit Hitchcock zu tun. Irgendwie gefällt es ihm mit unserer Tendenz zu spielen, diese Ahnung zu vervollständigen, dass uns die Gebäude ansprechen. Wir stellen uns dann vor, dass jemand hinter der Gardine steckt. Hinter einem geschlossenen Vorhang. Und das machen wir eigentlich die ganze Zeit mit jedem, der uns begegnet."
(René Pollesch)

finden Eingang in diese Arbeiten. Die vielgestaltigen opulenten Bühnenbilder von Bert Neumann, wie zuletzt das riesige Schiff in der Schiffbauhalle, oder lebenswerte Sprechchöre, beides in „Hereinl Hereinl Ich atme euch einl", prägen sein „Theater ohne Repräsentation". Im ständigen Rollen- und Identitätswechsel erzählen die Spieler seine Geschichte, sondern verhandeln Fragen nach Liebe, Arbeit und dem Subjekt in Zeiten des Kapitalismus. Durch Sprachwitz gepaart mit revanzigen Auftritten suchen die Spieler auf der Bühne ständig sich selbst, sind im falschen Bühnenbild oder verlieren sich in einem Chor.

René Pollesch arbeitet auch an der Volksbühne Berlin, am Burgtheater Wien, am Deutschen Schauspielhaus Hamburg, an den Münchner Kammerspielen und am Schauspiel Stuttgart seit Jahren kontinuierlich und ist im Zürcher Programm eine feste Grösse. „Ein Liebhaberstück" ist seine sechste Arbeit in Zürich.

Seit Jahren prägt René Pollesch, geboren 1962, als Regisseur und Autor ein unverwechselbares Theaterfondschl. Seine Inszenierungen, die er ausgehend von seinen eigenen Texten erarbeitet, entstehen immer in enger Zusammenarbeit mit dem Ensemble und haben schon wegen ihrer humorvollen, überbordenden Bilderwelt und Sprechchöre Kultstatus erworben. Pop-, Theorie- und Boulevard-Elemente

---

Die Jungfrau von Orleans

Pfauen
Premiere am 25. September 2015

von Friedrich Schiller

mit einem Text von Peter Stamm

Regie: Stephan Kimmig
Bühne: Katja Haß
Kostüme: Johanna Pfau
Musik: Michael Verhovec
Video: Julian Krubasik und Lambert Strehlke

1429, während des Hundertjährigen Kriegs zwischen England und Frankreich, erscheint ein lothringisches Bauernmädchen, Johanna, mit göttlichen Sendungsbewusstsein im französischen Lager und führt an der Spitze des Heers der Franzosen zum Sieg. Sie befreit die Stadt Orleans, vertreibt die Engländer aus weiten Teilen des Landes und bringt den Dauphin Karl VII zur Krönung nach Reims. Ein einfaches Hirtenmädchen als Freiheitskämpferin und Gotteskriegerin? Für die einen Fluch und Verderben, für die anderen Segen und glückliche bzw. göttliche Fügung. Schiller war fasziniert von der zauberhaften, legendenhaften Geschichte der Jeanne d'Arc, der Nationalheldin der Franzosen wurde. Bei ihm ist sie nicht einfach Fahnenträgerin; sie tötet eigenhändig und in göttlicher Mission. Sie erscheint aus dem Nichts, verschwindet ins Nichts. Die Auftritte dieser Gotteskriegerin berühren das Numinose, das Unerklärliche und Schicksalhafte. Mit ihrem Todesspektakel verbreitet sie mythischen Schrecken, wie man es vielleicht aus den Geschichten des Alten Testaments kennt. Erst als sie dem englischen Heerführer Lionel begegnet und sich verliebt, versagt ihr die Kraft. Sie schreitet mit ihrem göttlichen Auftrag, kann nicht mehr töten. Das „Wundermädchen" ist verletzt, weil sie liebt.

Schiller zeigt in seiner „romantischen Tragödie" von 1801 den Weg eines Menschen, vom „blinden Werkzeug Gottes" zum handelnden und fühlenden Menschen, der seine

unvermeidbare Schuld erkennt, und den Konflikt zwischen göttlichem Auftrag und menschlichem Gefühl, zwischen Pflicht und Neigung.

Stephan Kimmig, geboren 1959 in Stuttgart, arbeitet u. a. am Deutschen Theater Berlin, an den Münchner Kammerspielen, am Wiener Burgtheater, am Staatstheater Stuttgart und an der Bayerischen Staatsoper München. Neben regelmässigen Einladungen zum Berliner Theatertreffen, darunter „Thyestes", „Nora" und „Maria Stuart", erhielt er u.a. den Wiener Nestroy-, den Rolf-Mares- und den Faust-Preis sowie – zusammen mit der Bühnenbildnerin Katja Haß – den Basf-Innovationspreis für zukunftsweisende Leistungen im Deutschen Schauspiel für „Maria Stuart". Mit seiner Inszenierung von „Jungfrau von Orleans" stellt er sich zum ersten Mal dem Zürcher Publikum vor.

Unterstützt von der Hans Imholz Stiftung

Pfauen
Premiere am 10. September 2015

von Henrik Ibsen

in einer Bearbeitung von Dietmar Dath

Regie: Stefan Pucher
Bühne: Barbara Ehnes
Kostüme: Annabelle Witt
Musik: Christopher Uhe
Video: Ute Schall

Ein Volksfeind

Der Arzt Thomas Stockmann fühlt sich aufgrund vermehrter Krankheitsfälle von Kurgästen in seiner Heimatstadt dazu veranlasst, Nachforschungen anzustellen. Die zeigen, dass Fäulnisstoffe aus einer naheliegenen Fabrik die örtlichen Bäder vergiften. Er macht seine Entdeckungen publik, fordert Massnahmen zur Behebung der Missstände und findet zunächst auch Zustimmung seitens der Bürger. Als sein Bruder, der Bürgermeister Peter Stockmann, jedoch aufzeigt, welche Verluste die Bäderanstalten und der Kurort zu tragen hätten, steht er zunehmend auf verlorenem Posten. Mit einer anklagenden, unversöhnlichen Ansprache verliert er sich auch die letzten Sympathien: Die Bürgerversammlung beschimpft ihn einen „Volksfeind".

Das Stück des norwegischen Dramatikers Henrik Ibsen aus dem Jahr 1883 ist eine gesellschaftskritische Anklage und Satire zugleich, eine Kampfansage an die bürgerliche Welt seiner Zeit, die Ibsen von einer Lebenslüge zerfressen sieht. Der Autor und Dramatiker Dietmar Dath erarbeitet die Zürcher Fassung.

Dath, ehemals Chefredakteur der Zeitschrift Spex sowie Feuilletonchef der FAZ, hat mit seinen Sachbüchern und seinen zahlreichen Romanen auf sich aufmerksam gemacht. Er ist bekennender Marxist und befragt in seinen Schriften unsere Art des Zusammenlebens in Form von Science-Fiction und Zukunftsszenarien.

Stefan Pucher, 1965 in Giessen geboren, konzipierte verschiedene Performance-Projekte, so am TAT in Frankfurt am Main und mit der britischen Gruppe „Gob Squad". Seit 1999 inszeniert er u. a. am Theater Basel, am Deutschen Schauspielhaus Hamburg, an der Volksbühne am Rosa-Luxemburg-Platz in Berlin, an den Münchner Kammerspielen sowie am Deutschen Theater Berlin. In Zürich hat er u. a. „Und eines Handlungsreisenden" von Arthur Miller (eingeladen zum Berliner Theatertreffen 2011), „Die Katze auf dem heissen Blechdach" von Tennessee Williams (2013) und „Woyzeck" von Georg Büchner (2014) auf die Bühne gebracht.

Unterstützt von Swiss Re

Homo faber

Pfauen
Premiere am 30. September 2016

nach dem Roman von Max Frisch

Regie Bastian Kraft
Bühne Peter Baur
Kostüme Sabin Fleck

„Gewohnt, immer in Bewegung zu sein, gewohnt, dass alles funktioniert – und zwar so, wie ich es will –, lese ich ‚Homo faber' und frage mich, ob nicht der ‚Fehler im System ich' ein Glücksfall ist, der Stillstand mich nach vorn bringt, der Sand im Getriebe die Maschine eigentlich befeuert."
Bastian Kraft

Die Notlandung eines Flugzeugs in der Wüste. Darin der Passagier Walter Faber, ein Schweizer Ingenieur mit einem unerschütterlich rationalistischen Weltbild – ein Mann über 50, der alles, was an Kunst, Liebe, Religion oder Schicksal nicht wissenschaftlich erklärbar ist, beiseite tut. Zwar ist auch die Begegnung in diesem Flugzeug mit Hermann, der ihn von seinen Plänen abbringt und zu seinem alten Freund Joachim in die Wüste führt, schon ein erstaunlicher Zufall. Ins Wanken gerät Walter Fabers Weltbild aber erst, als er sich gezwungen sieht, vor sich selbst und seiner ehemaligen Geliebten Hanna über die jüngste Vergangenheit Bericht abzulegen. Dazu kommt es, weil er auf einem Schiff nach New York nach Frankreich eine junge Frau kennenlernt, die ihn an Hanna erinnert: Sabeth. Er lässt seine Reisepläne fallen und begleitet die junge Frau in jugendlicher Verliebtheit quer durch Europa nach Athen. Trotz aller Indizien begreift er nicht, dass er mit seiner eigenen Tochter kokettiert – Hannas Tochter, die sie, kurz nachdem er sie verlassen hatte, zur Welt brachte.

Den als Rechenschaftsbericht verfassten Roman schreibt Max Frisch, selbst Architekt und Literat, 1957 und spiegelt gerade in Fabers Versuch einer genauen Rekonstruktion der Geschehnisse sein Scheitern, die Welt und sein Leben als blosse Addition der Fakten zu begreifen.

Der Regisseur Bastian Kraft, geboren 1980, beschäftigt sich nach „Andorra" von Max Frisch (Schiffbau/Box 2016) in Zürich zum zweiten Mal mit diesem Schweizer Autor.

Unterstützt vom Förderer-Circle des Schauspielhauses

Lena Schwarz

Jirka Zett

14

Extra

Pfauen/Kammer
Close Up

PEER.GYNT
(in Planung)

Eine szenische Lesung mit Musik und Live-Zeichnung

Mit Hans Kremer (Wort und Spiel), Esther Schöpf (Violine und Gesang), Norbert Groh (Akkordeon und Klavier), Isabelle Krötsch (Live-Zeichnung und Gesamtgestaltung)

Ein szenisches Experiment über Wahrheit und Lüge, Wirklichkeit und Projektion und die Transzendenz der Liebe. Basis sind zwei Klassiker: Henrik Ibsens „Peer Gynt" und Edvard Griegs „Suiten zu Peer Gynt" sowie seine für das Theaterstück konzipierte Bühnenmusik inklusive Tänze. Beide Werke werden in der Installation „Laut-Malen" mit theatralischen Mitteln erkundet. Die klassischen Partituren bilden Inspiration und Leitfaden. Die Begegnungen von Wort, Bild und Klang werden durch Improvisation erweitert und eröffnen so neue Perspektiven auf den Stoff, der in seiner Abhandlung über das herrschende materialistische Weltbild aktueller ist denn je.

Das Kollektiv um Hans Kremer nimmt Ibsens Thesen: „Mensch sei du selbst" und „Mensch sei dir selbst genug" auf die Spur. Das Epos ist auch eine Hommage an die Kraft der Vorstellung und die Magie des Erzählens. Die Imagination des Betrachters wird durch das skizzenhafte Arbeiten zum eigentlichen Akteur. Gleichzeitig hinterfragt dieses Werkstatt das Denkers das im Stück thematisierte Kopftheater, das für viele Menschen unserer Zeit Realität geworden ist.

Pfauen/Kammer
Close Up

Hans Schleif

Eine Spurensuche mit Matthias Neukirch

Regie Julian Klein

Hans Schleif war Architekt und Archäologe, renommierter Wissenschaftler, Professor für antike Baukunst, Familienvater und ranghohes Mitglied der SS. Sein Enkel, Schauspieler und Ensemblemitglied Matthias Neukirch, begibt sich auf die Suche nach der Biografie seines Grossvaters. Er beginnt eine Recherche in Dokumenten, Archiven und den Erinnerungen der Familie, die ihn mitten in die Gegenwart und zu sich selbst führt.

Der sehr persönliche Soloabend, der gleichzeitig auf bizarre Art antike Mythen, Holocaust und Wunderwaffen miteinander verknüpft, macht Geschichte unmittelbar greifbar. Die Produktion aus dem Jahre 2011 tourt europaweit und wurde für den Friedrich-Luft-Preis nominiert.

„Nun wird's wohl klappen, wie immer in wirklich guten Zeiten gilt die Tugend!"
aus „Hans Schleif"

58

Michael Neuenschwander

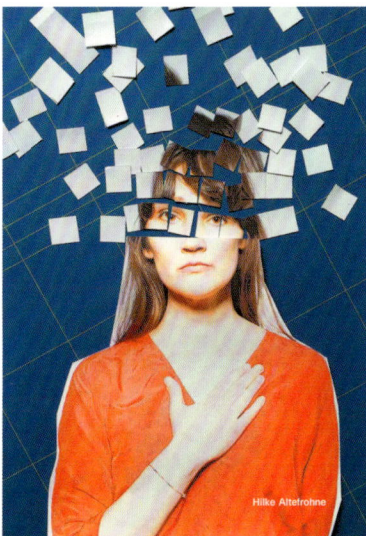
Hilke Altefrohne

Schiffbau/Box
Uraufführung am 15. Oktober 2016

Texte von Jacques Brel

zusammengestellt und übersetzt von Yves Binet

Mit André Jung

Regie Werner Düggelin
Bühne und Kostüme Raimund Bauer

„Parce que monter en voiture c'est dangereux pour la santé; vivre c'est dangereux pour la santé; faire l'amour c'est dangereux pour la santé; courir c'est très mauvais pour la santé et dire des rêves c'est très mauvais pour la santé morale. Tout est extrêmement mauvais pour la santé …"
Jacques Brel

Mit 49 Jahren stirbt der belgische Chansonnier Jacques Brel in einem Pariser Krankenhaus. Mehr als 10 Jahre zuvor gibt der unangepasste Lebenskünstler seinen letzten triumphalen Bühnenauftritt. Danach zieht er sich, obwohl ihm Paris zu Füssen liegt, auf die Südseeinsel Hiva Ova zurück. Bis zu seinem Tod ist er ein rastloser Kämpfer und bekriegt wie sein liebster Romanheld Don Quixote im Namen der Träume und der Zärtlichkeit wider die Windmühlen des Lebens: das Mittelmass, das Unbewegliche, die Bourgeoisie und ihr Geld. Seine Lieder bleiben Hymnen der Zweifler, Unangepassten und Gestrandeten.

In zahlreichen Interviews legt er Zeugnis über sein Leben ab. Sie lesen sich als widersprüchliche Suche nach sich selbst: in endlosen Ausschweifungen über Ermüdigungen, Niederlagen, Krankheit und Tod rechnet ein Mann mit den Zumutungen ab, die das Leben für ihn bereithält. Gleichzeitig sind sie Liebeserklärungen an das Leben, verglichen mit Brels orkanhaften Bühnenauftritten, in denen er seine Zuhörer in wildem Tempo in Euphorie versetzte.

Werner Düggelin kreiert aus Jacques Brels Worten den Erinnerungsraum eines Nomaden als Monolog für den Schauspieler André Jung. Seit Jahrzehnten arbeiten Düggelin und Jung miteinander, so auch im Schauspielhaus, wo u.a. „Endspiel" von Samuel Beckett, „Bunbury" von Oscar Wilde und „Volpone" von Ben Jonson entstanden sind.

17

Marie Rosa Tietjen

Pfauen/Kammer
Premiere Februar 2017

Zündels Abgang

nach dem Roman von Markus Werner

Regie Zino Wey
Bühne und Kostüme Davy van Gerven
Musik Benjamin Brodbeck

„‚Zündels Abgang' verstehe ich als eine poetische Beschreibung eines Unwohlseins, die subtile Beobachtung eines Ausbruchs. Eine Spurensuche nach einem Menschen, der sich irgendwann verliert. Eine Spurensuche nach einem Selbst, das sich irgend wann aufzulösen beginnt."
Zino Wey

„Dem Weltgeschehen schenk ich Interesse und Wut, aber ich glaube, es pfeift darauf." Konrad Zündel ist Mitte 30, Lehrer und verheiratet. Besonders glücklich macht ihn das nicht, besonders unglücklich aber auch nicht. Das Dilemma beginnt mit Zündels Überzeugung von der Untreue seiner Frau Magda. Nach fünf Jahren Ehe kriselt es. Ein getrennter Sommerurlaub soll Distanz schaffen, soll klären, soll helfen.

Nach seinem missglückten Versuch einer Griechenlandreise, die er wegen eines Pannenlusts eines Schneidezahns abbrechen muss, unternimmt Zündel einen neuen Anlauf. Ein Zug bringt ihn nach Genua. Dort gerät er in abenteuerlich-kriminelle und absurd-erklärliche Situationen und in zweideutige Etablissements. Er begegnet Ganoven und leichten Damen, trinkt zu viel Alkohol, schläft kaum und erlebt lauter Seltsamkeiten. Zündel ist von der Schlechtigkeit der Welt überzeugt und geniesst sie aber in vollen Zügen. „Die Wirklichkeit – seelenruhig fürchterlicher und unbeschreiblicher werdend von Tag zu Tag zwingt entweder zum totalen Rückzug oder zum jauchzenden Anarchismus."

Nur noch selten denkt er an Magda und an Zuhause. Der Strudel, der ihn ergriffen hat, lässt ihn nicht mehr los, zieht ihn weiter weg von sich fort, bis er schliesslich einen Entschluss fällt und verschwindet.

Das tragikomische Debüt des Schweizer Schriftstellers Markus Werner, dessen poetische und stimmungsvolle Inszenierung an Philipp Löhles „Kollaps" letzte Spielzeit in der Kammer zu sehen war, arbeitet u.a. an Nationaltheater Mannheim, an den Münchner Kammerspielen und an der Kaserne Basel.

49

Hafenkran Zürich
Homage to the land art sculpture "Der Hafenkran" (2014–2015) by Zürich-Transit-Maritim (Jan Morgenthaler, Barbara Roth, Martin Senn and Fariba Sepehrnia).

2014

BD

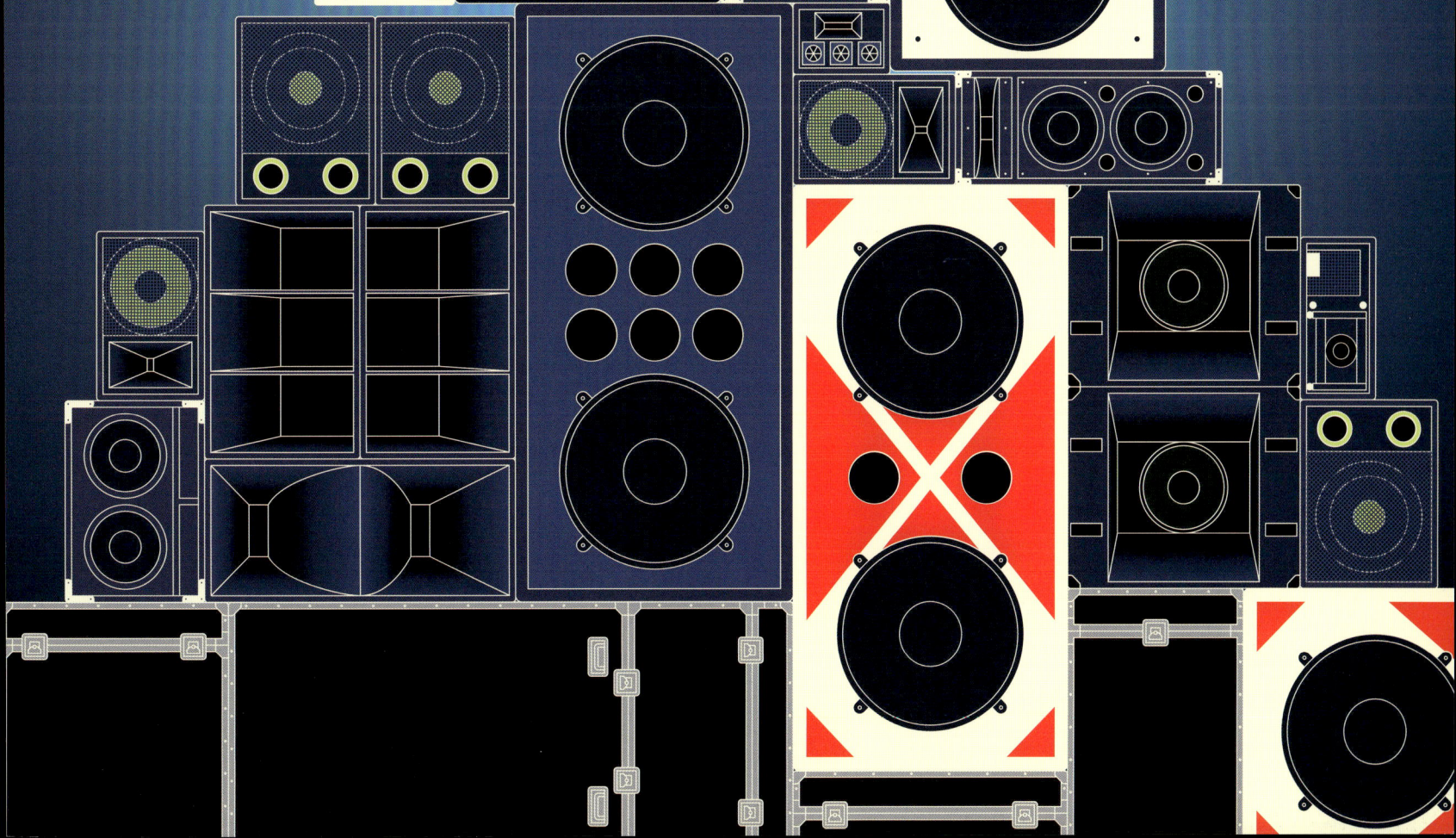

VISION Festival –
Flatline remix
Posters, flyers and
advertisements.
297 × 420 mm
420 × 594 mm
594 × 841 mm

Client:
DekaDance

2011

Rhythm of 2021
New Years card
148 × 210 mm

2020 / 2021

Right page:
Der Elektrische Mann
CD and single sleeve
artworks

Client:
Ane Hebeisen,
Christian Sommerhalder

2019

rhythm of 2021

DER ELEKTRISCHE ELEKTRISCHE MANN

MUSIK
MUSIK MUSIK

SAG MIR WAS DU DENKST DENKST DENKST DENKST
ELEKTRISCHE MANN DER DENKST

WIR GEBEN NICHTS NICHTS
ELEKTRISCHE MANN DER HER

MUSIK MUSIK MUSIK
ELEKTRISCHE MANN DER MUSIK

MUSIKMUSIKMUSIKMUSIKMUSIKMUSIKMUSIKMUSIK
D.E.M.

BD WESTWWORK
BCDEFGHIJKLMNOPQRSTUVWXYZ
abcdefghijklmnopqrstuuwxyz
#1234567890%&¥$€£□®□I?
ÇÑÃÉÖÚÅ®Đ£þÆ□□°*™

Right page:
DJ Krush
Concert poster
420×594mm

Illustration by 冬奇

Client:
Reitschule
Dachstock, Bern

2018

Above:
BD Westwork
Typedifferent font

2018

www.typedifferent.com

Right:
Crypto Gin
Packaging design

Client:
Christoph Jenny

2018

Unrealised

CRYPTOGIN

MINED FOR EARLY ADOPTERS

ICH BIN EIN BLINDTEXT. BLIND VON GEBURT AN. UND ES HAT SEINE ZEIT GEDAUERT, BIS ICH BEGRIFFEN HABE, WAS ES BEDEUTET, EIN BLINDER TEXT ZU SEIN MAN MACHT KEINEN SINN. VIELFACH WIRD MAN SOGAR BESCHNITTEN, AUS DEM ZUSAMMENHANG GERISSEN, OFT NICHT MAL GELESEN. ABER BIN ICH EIN SCHLECHTER TEXT DESWEGEN? GEWISS, ICH WEISS, DASS ICH NIEMALS DIE CHANCE HABEN WERDE, IN DEN FÜHRENDEN ZEITUNGEN ZU ERSCHEINEN.

BATCH# BOTTL# BLEND# PYEAR# DISTILLER:

42% / 700ML

CRAFTED BY DARKNETDISTILLERY.COM | CRYPTOGIN.NET

DESTILLAT AUS AGRARROHSTOFFEN IN 1. QUALITÄT, DOPPELT GEBRANNT UND MAZERIERT MIT WACHOLDER-BEEREN, FRISCHEM ROSMARIN UND 7 WEITEREN BOTANICS. DESTILLIERTER GIN GEMÄSS EG-NR. 110/2008/20

BD:213

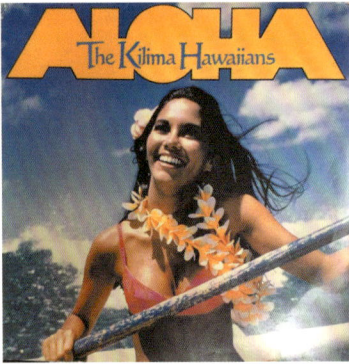

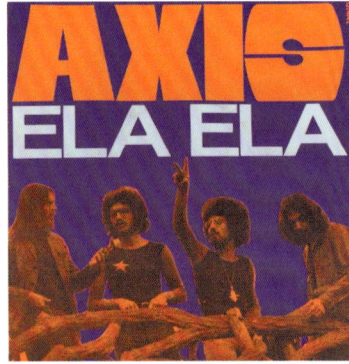

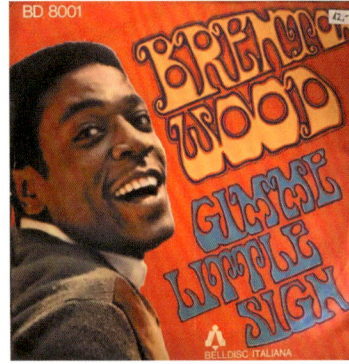

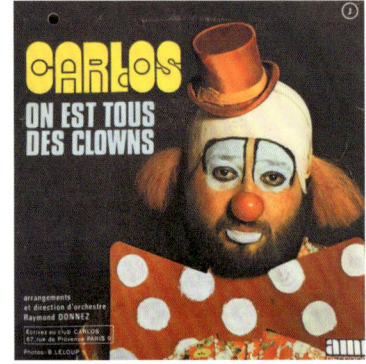

Fonts From The Flea Market
is an ongoing discovery of typefaces on used 7" vinyl singles found and photographed by Lopetz at flea markets and second-hand shops.

In the days when music was still sold as a physical, tangible product, record sleeves provided original typefaces with a great platform to catch the potential record buyer's attention.

Hunting down those imaginative type designs since 2005 became a source of inspiration for Büro Destruct's own type-foundry "typedifferent.com".

The collection currently holds over 1000 images and counting.

Thanks for tagging the typefaces: Florian Hardwig (Fontsinuse.com)

Browse the collection on Flickr:

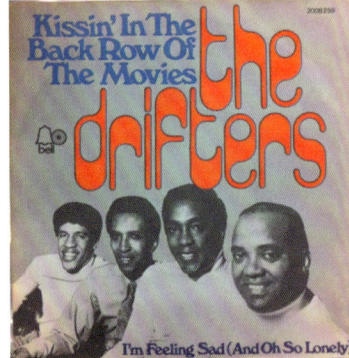

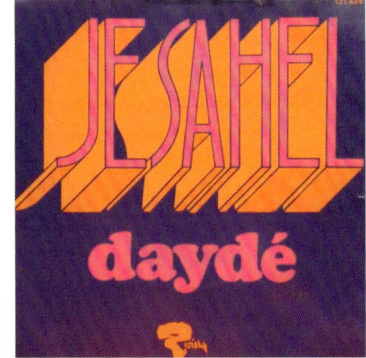

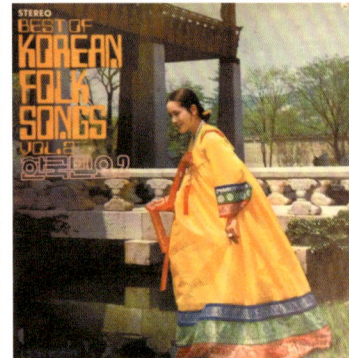

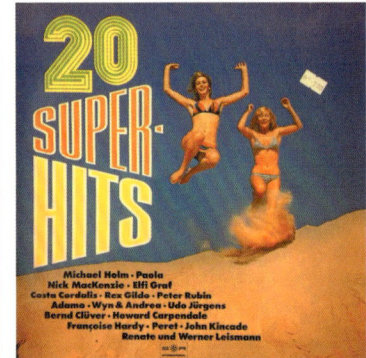

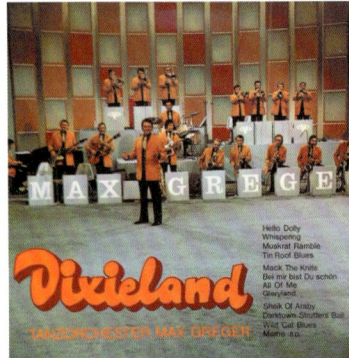

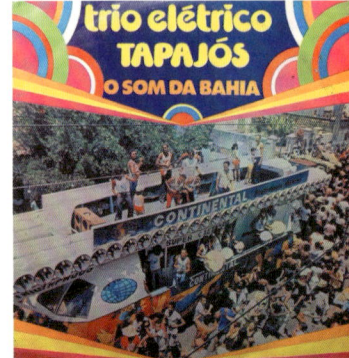

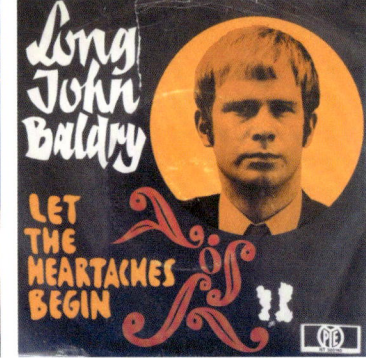

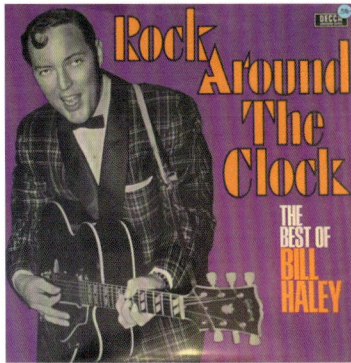
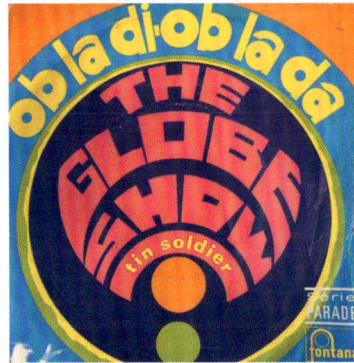

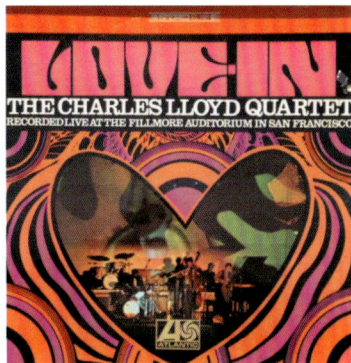

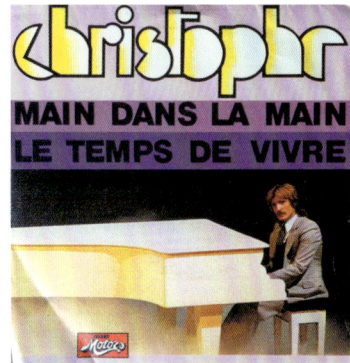

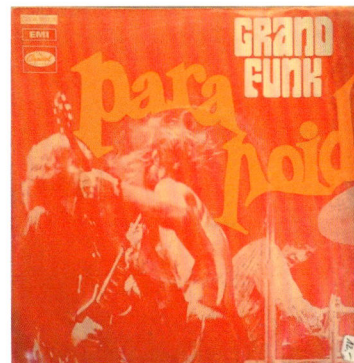
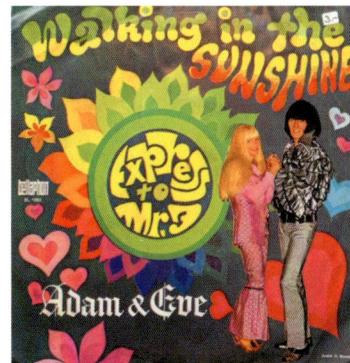

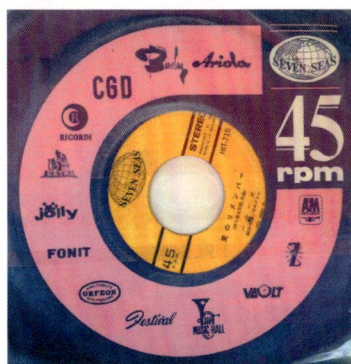

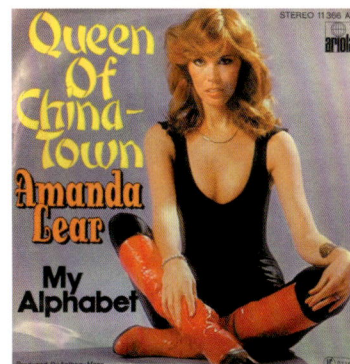

**Ka Moser –
Die Stimme des Klaviers
ist Musik**
CD sleeve artwork

Client:
Ka Moser

2014

Unpublished

Züri West
Concert flyer

Client:
Reitschule Dachstock,
Bern

2001

**Kids pick things up so easily.
Colds. Viruses. Japanese**
Poster design for V&A Museum
of Childhood UK.

Client:
AMV BBDO London

2013

Unpublished

Shisha
Flyer

Client:
sfa/ispa, National competence
center for prevention, research
and knowledge transfer in the
field of addiction

2008

Left:
Herbst Märit
Market-flyer, internship
collaboration with Nathan
Tomaschett

Client:
Stiftung Bächtelen

2019

Right:
Serigraphie Uldry
Postcard

Client:
Serigraphie Uldry

2018

**Balduin –
She's The One**
Demotape cover

Client:
Balduin

2021

Blues Horror Brigade – Bubbles
Remix single sleeve

Client:
Blues Horror Brigade

2010

Weiterbildung
Typographic visual
for a shopper bag.

Client:
Universität Bern

2019

Unpublished

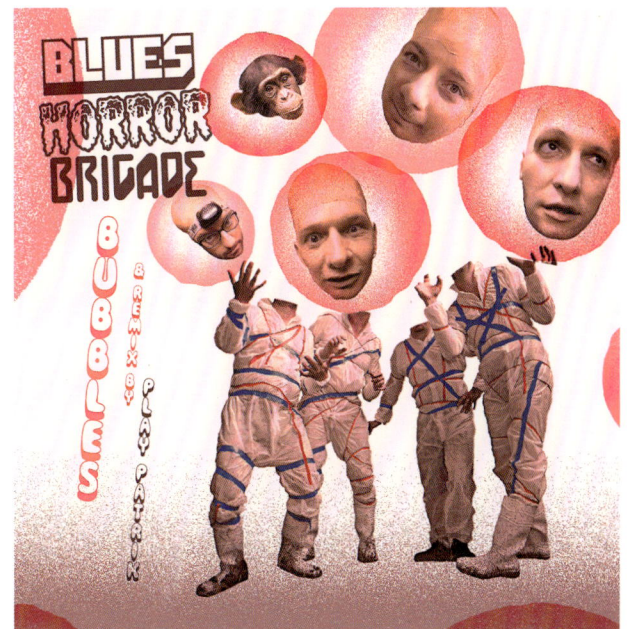

UMWELT
NACHHALTIGKEIT
GESELLSCHAFT

WIRTSCHAFT
MANAGEMENT
VERWALTUNG

RECHT
POLITIK

PSYCHOLOGIE
SEELSORGE
THEOLOGIE

BILDUNG
KULTUR
SPORT

ICT
DATA
WISSENSCHAFT

GESUNDHEIT
MEDIZIN

u^b

_b_
UNIVERSITÄT
BERN

WWW.
WEITER
BILDUNG.
UNIBE.CH

Schlauer Fuchs
Branding character design and
cluster icons for the further
education programme of the
University of Bern.

Client:
Zentrum für universitäre
Weiterbildung ZUW

2019–2021

BD:219

Kitchener
Various shop event flyers
and stickers.
148×105 mm
210×105 mm
120×120 mm

Client:
Kitchener, Bern

2016–2019

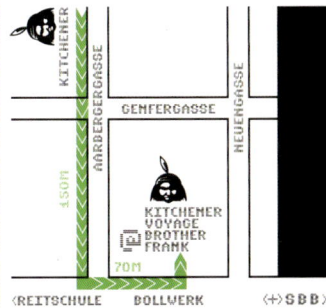

6./7.
AUGUST
2009
Im
Schwellenmätteli
Bern
WEINE GENIESSEN AN DER BERNER RIVIERA
vinaare
DIE
ZWEITÄGIGE
VERANSTALTUNG
RUND UM WEIN,
GENUSS UND
BEGEGNUNG

11./12.
AUGUST
2011
VINAARE
2011
WEINE GENIESSEN AN DER BERNER RIVIERA
IM SCHWELLENMÄTTELI BERN

15 & 16
AUGUST
2013
vinaare
WEINE GENIESSEN AN DER BERNER RIVIERA
IM SCHWELLENMÄTTELI BERN
MIT FOLGENDEN WINZERN:
WWW.CULTIVINO.CH/VINAARE

Vin
Aare
Alte Feuerwehr Viktoria
29. & 30. August 2015

Left:
Vinaare
Wine event posters
420 × 594 mm
297 × 420 mm

Client: Cultivino

2009–2015

This page:
Aus uns ist nichts geworden
Book cover illustration

Published by Verlag X-Time

Author and client:
Michael Sasdi

2018

AUS UNS IST NICHTS GEWORDEN

Progr Flag
Flag for the 10 years jubilee
of Progr. Based on the Progr
logo, it represents the broad
activity field in the artistic
center and cultural hub of Bern.
1500 × 1500 mm

Client:
PROGR / Ro*

2014

Yasuni
Illustration for the magazine
of Zurich Financial Services.
220 × 285 mm

Client:
Deep, Creative Design
Agency, London

2011

WeLove
Clubnight flyer
105 × 148 mm

Client:
Ferenz Poor

2013

The Stickerdoor
Internet-project with hand made stickers from street artists from all over the world, mixed with BD and other stickers.
900 × 2130 mm

Photo:
Nadia Schweizer

2005–2021

L'Heure Bleue
Artwork for a concert poster.

Client:
Mich Gerber

2020

L'HEURE
BLEUE
MICH
GERBER

Qoniak – Mutatio
LP sleeve artwork

Published by
Everest Records

Client:
Qoniak

2020

A1> SCOUL   4:42
A2> COAC   5:06
A3> IPSUM   3:34
A4> BAOBOB   5:08

B1> ROOIN   7:02
B2> QO   3:36
B3> GAUDENS   3:51
B4> BOKAL   4:45

Lionel Friedli / drums
Vincent Membrez / keys

Recorded at Artefax Studios /
Lausanne / by Antoine Etter

Mixed by David Odlum

Mastered by April Golden /
Golden Mastering / Ventura California

All compositions by Vincent Membrez

Avec le soutien de:
Family and friends: Matu, Jona, Estelle and Aline
Service de la culture de la Ville de Bienne
Swisslos - Culture Canton de Berne
Pro Helvetia- Fondation suisse pour la culture
Migros-Kulturprozent

No download code needed. Visit www-hummus-records.com
and download this album for free.

www.qoniakmusic.ch

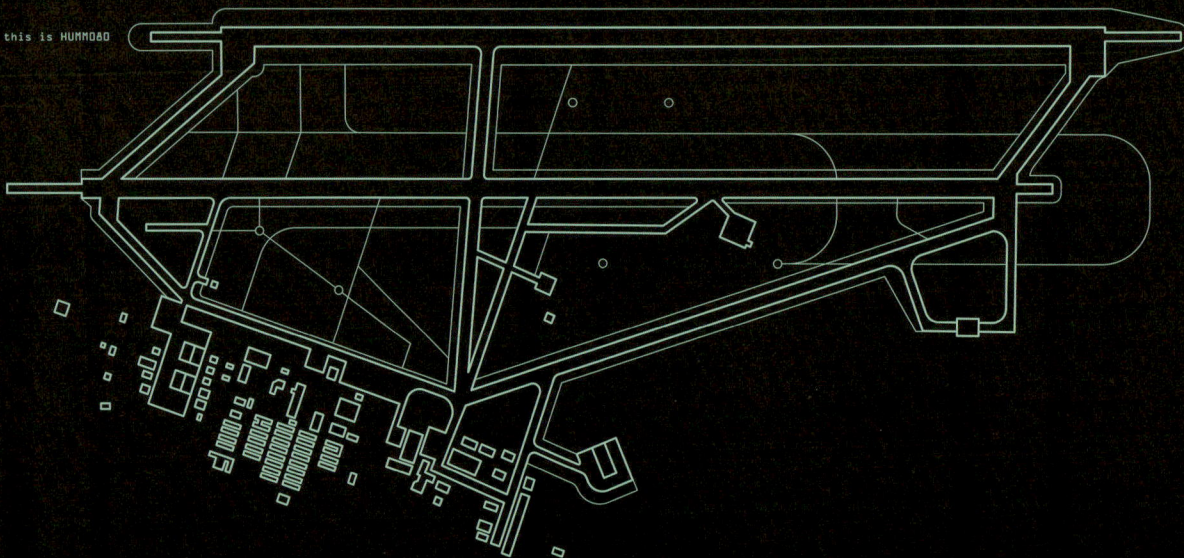

QONIAK

MUTATIO

Salzhaus
Poster
895 × 1280 mm

Client:
Salzhaus,
Winterthur

2014

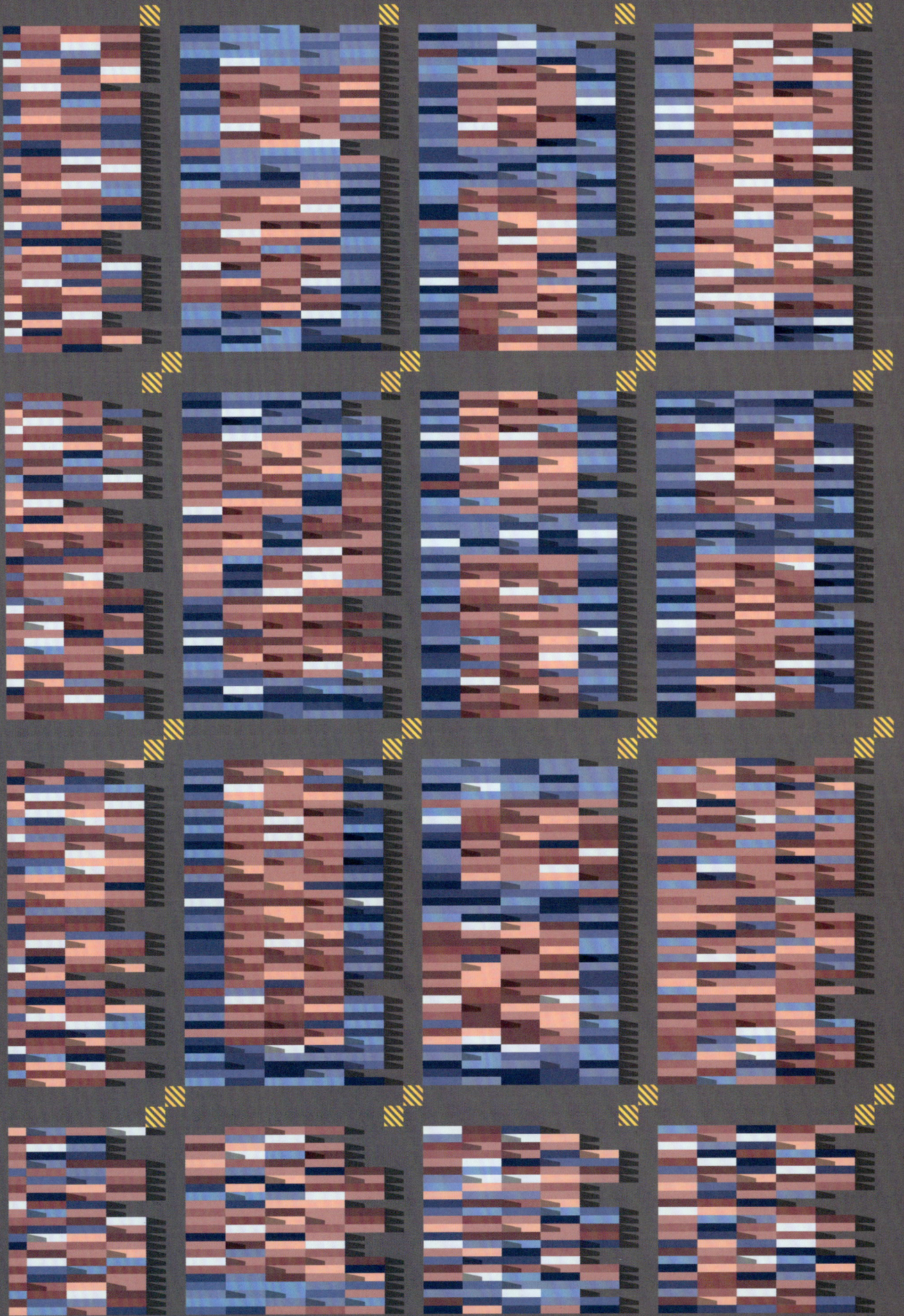

XA1

65870933 88001122

N
L

10

Form:uLA: Bryan Cantley

MECHUDZU

New Rhetorics for Architecture

nsfw
4
hm

REE 2-SS

REE -5-

NEW 6-38

Mechudzu
Editorial design for the book
Mechudzu by Form:uLA:
Bryan Cantley.
180 × 210 mm

Client:
RIEA.ch Research Institute for
Experimental Architecture

2011

RIEAch Research Institute for Experimental Architecture

Springer Wien New York

BD:232

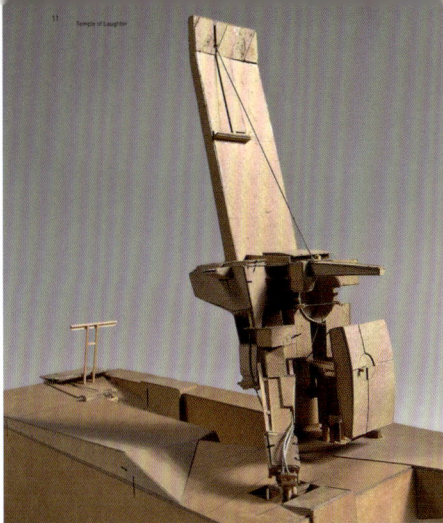

14

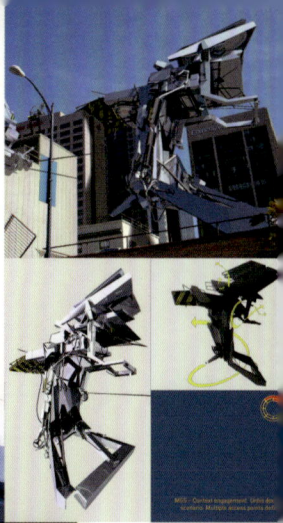

MCE: Contact engagement. Ortho devices/mods. Multiple actionesc points defined.

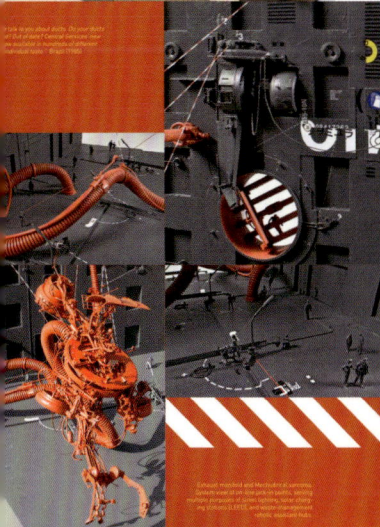

21

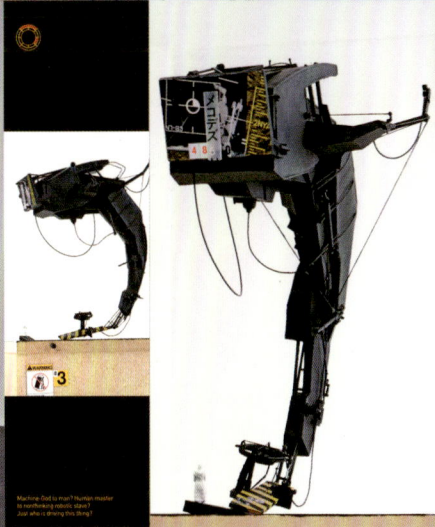

Machine-God is man? Human master to reinforcing robotic slave? Just who is driving this thing?

25

Temple of Architecture ... Church of the Machine. Will you be an observer or art agent? Are you input or output? A new way to get "saved"? Celebrate? Wash away your sins then? Just ...

30

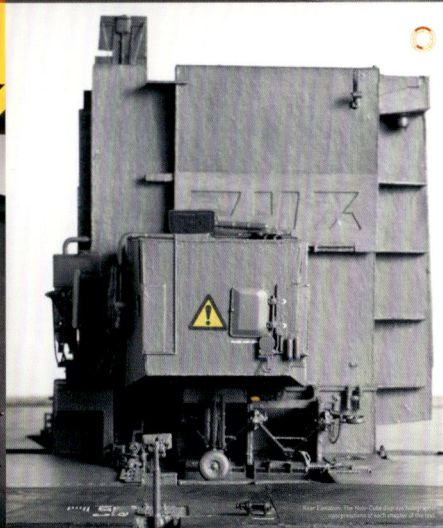

Rear Elevation. The Holo-Cube displays holographic reprogramming of each chapter of the text.

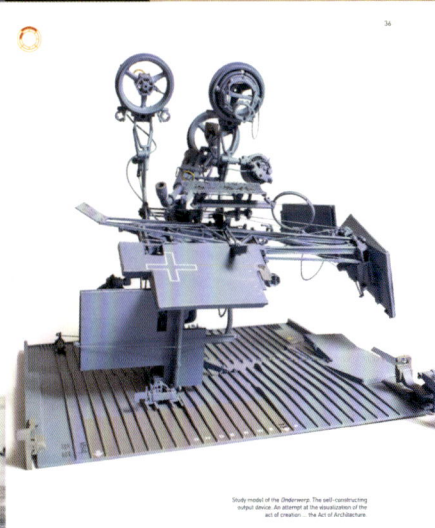

34

Study model of the Orderwerp. The self-constructing output device. An attempt at the visualization of the act of creation ... the Art of Architecture.

92

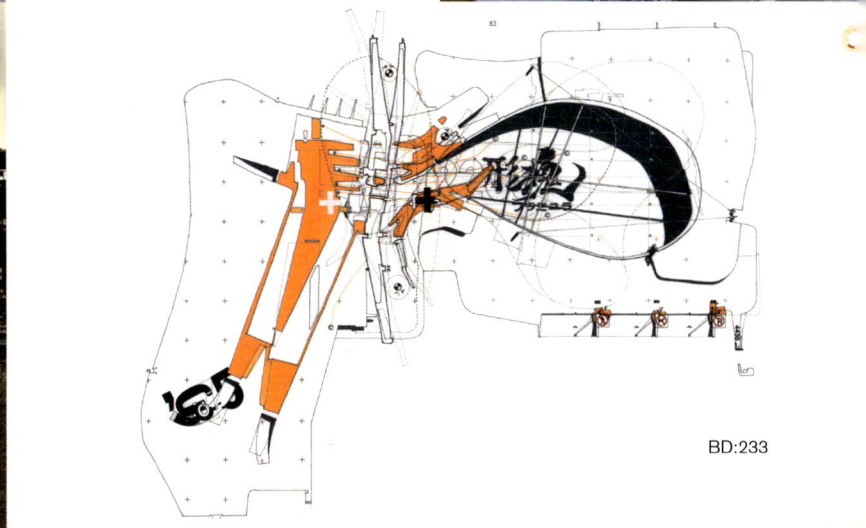

83

JAPAN 2019

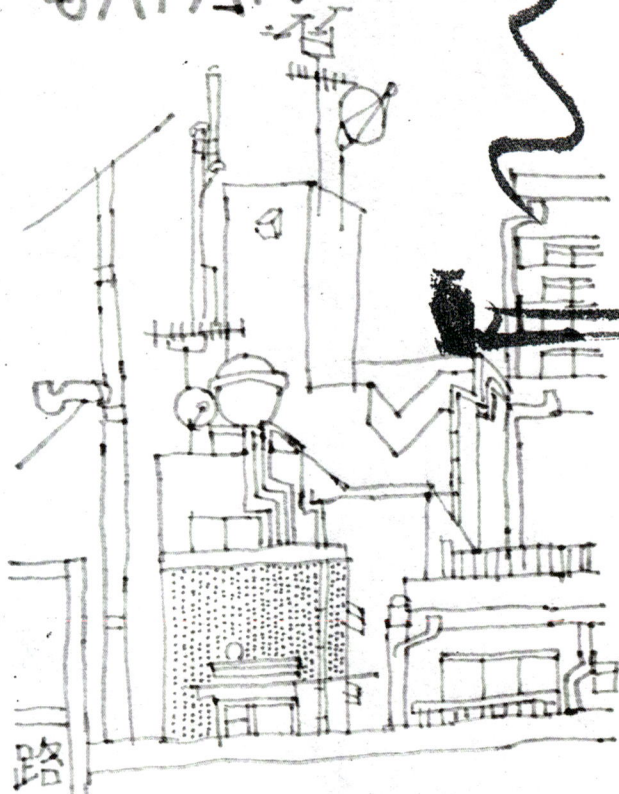

AirBnB うぐいすだに 替/2019 ロピ

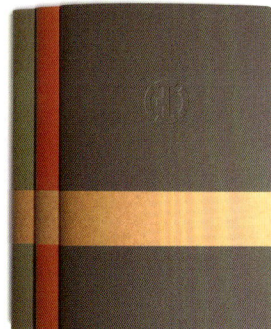

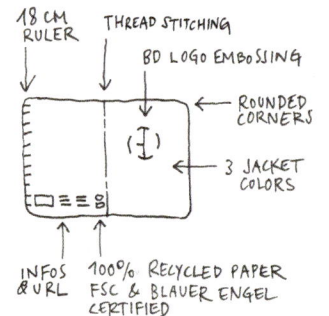

Scribbles made in Japan and Italy
View from the Airbnb and Kissaten in Uguisudani, Tokyo, Japan. At the beach in Borgio Verezzi & Finalpia, Liguria, Italy.

2016–2019

BD Sketchbooklet
Design and production of BD Sketchbooklets.

The form and function of the Sketchbooklet fits the needs of scribbling experienced at our studio over the past twenty years.

Produced with our local partners in Bern, Switzerland.

2016

www.sketchbooklet.com

Mario Batkovic … Introspectio

**Mario Batkovic –
Introspectio**
CD & LP sleeve artwork

Published by
Invada Records, UK

Client:
Mario Batkovic

2021

THE ERORR IS A GIFT

Bureau de Struct

coïncidence délibérée

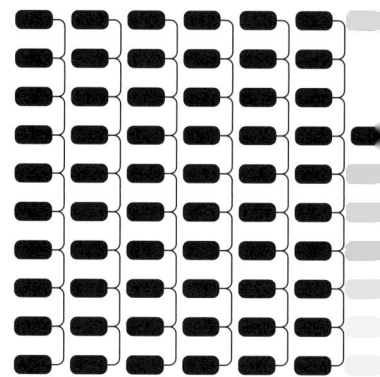

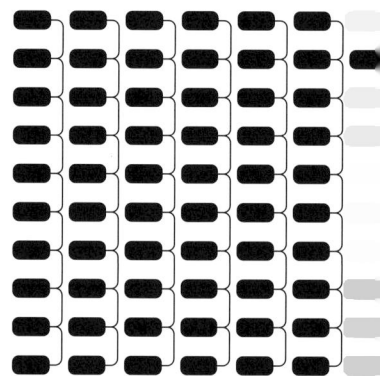

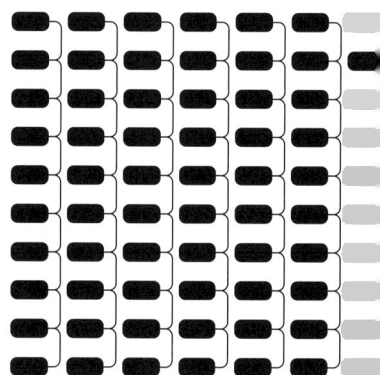

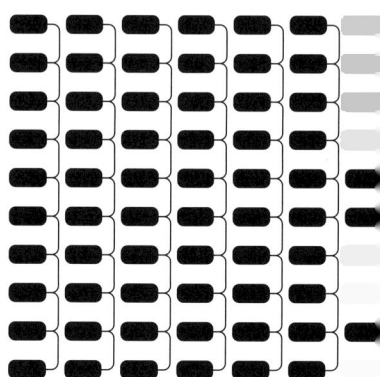

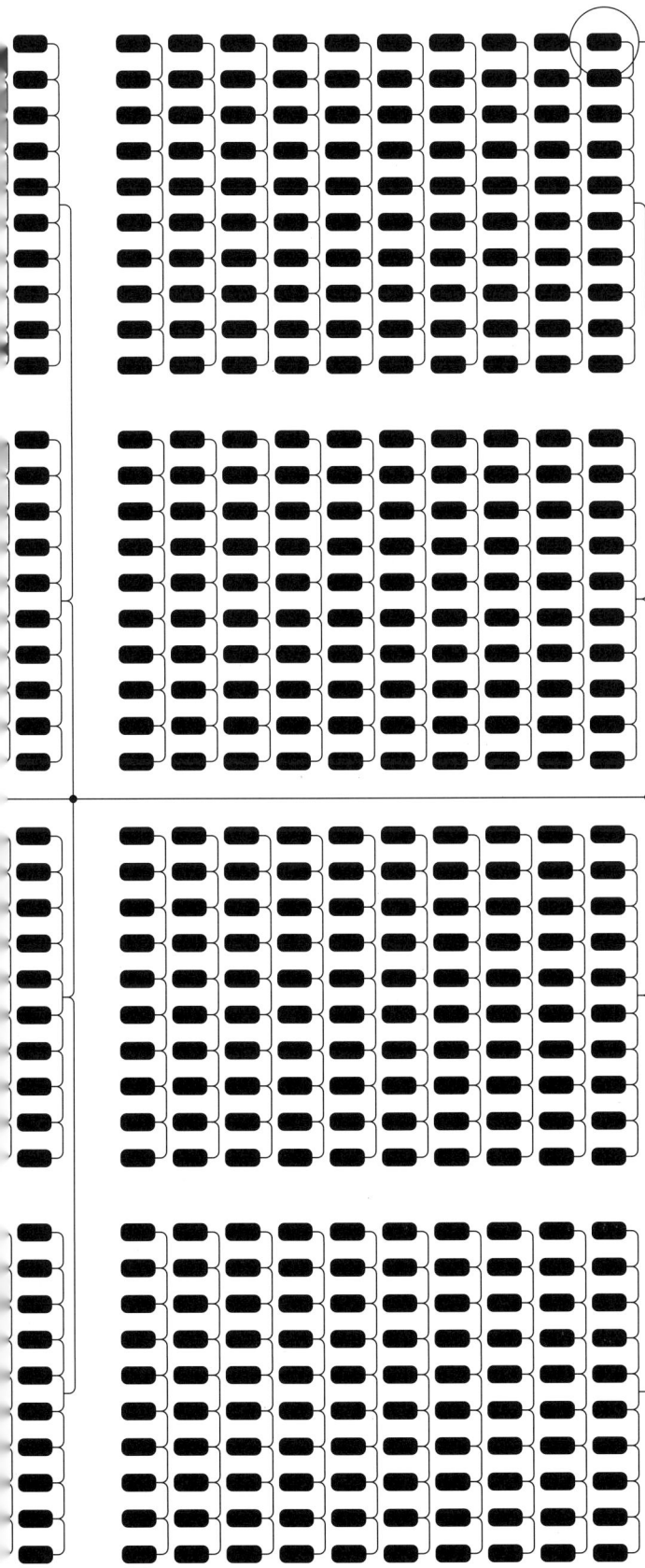

1PS

4PS

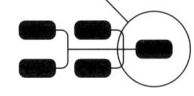

1600PS

Out of Scale

2021

PLAKATBAU
BD Plakatbau 1995

electrobazar
BD Electrobazar 1995

ELSIDE
BD Elside 1995

MEDLED
BD MedLed 1995

POKEMON
BD Pkany 1995

POCCER
BD Poccer 1995

dippey
BD Dippey 1995

BROCKELMANN
BD Brockelmann 1995

RatterBit
BD RatterBit 1995

FOXER
BD Foxer 1995

Ticket
BD Ticket 1995

brick
BD Brick 1996

cluster
BD Cluster 1996

Fazer
BD Fazer 1996

Globus
BD Globus 1996

LODEL FILLER
BD LodelFiller 1996

Rocket 70
BD Rocket70 1996

Billet
BD Billet 1996

CONSOLE
BD Console 1997

Lo-Fi
BD Lo-Fi 1997

kristalla
BD Kristalla 1996

CONSOLE
BD Console Remix 1997

eject
BD Eject 1998

Dutch
BD Ejen Kontinox 1998

SPICYFRUITS
BD SpicyFruits 1998

AcidBoyz
BD AcidBoyz 1998

Solaris
BD Solaris 1998

DOOMED
BD Doomed 1999

Craut
BD Craut 1999

STEREOTYPE
BD Stereotype 1999

BDR MONO
BD Mono 1999

alustar
BD Alustar 1999

ASCIIMAX
BD AsciiMax 1999

GalaQuadra
BD GalaQuadra 1999

Rainbow
BD Rainbow 2000

RELAUNCH
BD Relaunch Katakana 2000

CYCLE
BD Relaunch 2000

WURST
BD Wurst 2000

DELAFRANCE
BD DelaFrance 2000

colonius
BD Colonius 2001

Tatami
BD Tatami 2001

balduin
BD Balduin 2001

Mustang
BD Mustang 2001

bankwell
BD Bankwell 2001

billeding
BD BillDing 2001

METER
BD Meter 2001

CashBox
BD CashBox 2001

Cash
BD Cash 2001

bd-alm
BD Alm 2001

HexaDes
BD HexaDes 2001

CENTRAL
BD Central 2002

orlando
BD Orlando 2002

Apotheke
BD Apotheke 2002

BAND
BD Band 2002

BD-HELL
BD Hell 2002

Endless
BD Endless 2002

SweetHome
BD SweetHome 2002

Ritmic
BD Ritmic 2002

jura
BD Jura 2002

NIPPORI
BD Nippori 2002

BONBON
BD BonBon 2002

AROMA
BD Aroma 2005

Zenith
BD Zenith 2005

NEBRASKA
BD Nebraska 2005

St. Moritz
BD St.Moritz 2003

Discount
BD Discount 2003

BREAKBEAT
BD Breakbeat 2003

bd Mann
BD Mann 2003

STALKER
BD Stalker 2003

GEMINIS
BD Geminis 2003

Burner
BD Burner 2003

bardust
BD Bardust 2003

elmax
BD Elmax 2003

circa
BD Sirca 2003

Ramen
BD Ramen 2003

wotka
BD Wotka 2003

VICTORIA
BD Victoria 2004

SPINNER
BD Spinner 2004

bernebeats
BD Bernebeats 2004

Unexpected
BD Unexpected 2004

DECKART
BD Deckart 2004

ELAutobus
BD ELAutobus 2004

EQUIPMENT
BD Equipment 2004

Designer
BD Designer 2004

ワカリマス
BD Wakarimasu 2004

EXTRAWURST
BD Extrawurst 2005

VARVADRY
BD Varvadry 2005

EMERALD
BD Emerald 2005

Varicolor
BD Varicolor 2005

Aquatico
BD Aquatico 2005

MANDARIN
BD Mandarin 2005

Polo Hofer
BD Polo 2005

beans
BD Beans 2005

Chantilly
BD Chantilly 2005

TINYFONT
BD TinyFont 2005

Kalinka
BD TinyRock 2005

BDR MONO 2006
BD Mono 2006

Jupiter
BD Jupiter 2006

PANZER
BD Panzer 2006

BD Pipe
BD Pipe 2006

TimesNewDigital
BD Time New Digital 2006

Radiograph
BD Radiograph 2007

Mother
BD Mother 2007

DEMON
BD Demon 2007

BERMUDA
BD Bermuda 2007

REITHALLE
BD Reithalle 2007

Fimo Outline
BD Fimo 2007

MALFAIRE
BD Malfaire 2007

SMOKER
BD Smoker 2007

VIEWMASTER
BD Viewmaster 2008

VIEWMASTER NEON
BD Viewmaster Neon 2008

MOTRA
BD Motra 2008

BROADBAND
BD Broadband 2008

SPACY 125
BD Spacy 125 2008

virtual
BD Virtual 2008

WURST DIRECTORS CUT
BD Wurst Directors Cut 2008

BDR A3MIX
BDR A3MIX 2009

Retrocentric
BD Retrocentric 2009

HITBIT
BD HitBit 2009

calamares
BD Calamares 2009

STONEHENGE
BD Stonehenge 2009

KAMERON
BD Kameron 2009

robotron
BD Robotron 2009

KINDI
BD Kindi 2009

algebra
BD Algebra 2009

OUTLINE
BD Outline 2009

UNFOLD
BD Unfold 2009

UNICORSE
BD Unicorse 2010

LAS PALMAS
BD Las Palmas 2010

TELEGRAPH
BD Telegraph 2010

nokio
BD Nokio 2010

CIRCO
BD Circo 2010

BD Stella
BD Stella 2010

BALDRIAN
BD Baldrian 2010

Plankton
BD Plankton 2010

EDDING
Edding050 2010

USINEKE
BD Nagumo Rism 2011

Ragout
BD Ragout 2011

NARANINO
Num Nino 2012

SCHABLONE
BD Schablone 2012

FLUKE
BD Fluke 2012 (1997)

RIK
BD Rik 2012 (1997)

20 Minuten
20 Minuten 2012

Destination
BD Destination 2012

SHOWLONG
BD Showlong 2015

GOOD WOOD
BD Good Wood 2015

PANKOW
BD Pankow 2015

STENCLER
BD Stencler 2015

JAYIN FONTA
BD Jayin Fonta 2015

Qualle
BD Qualle 2016

tribler
BD Tribler 2016

BarbedUx
BD Barbedux 2015

fontaberto
BD Fontaberto 2015

MONSTER
BD Monster La Sonz 2015

KICKROM
BD Kickrom 2016

MATROSE
BD Matrose 2017

WESTWORK
BD Westwork 2018

MICRON FONT
BD MicronFont 2019

T AUTUMN
BD Micronfutura 2019

Aubergin
BD Aubergin 2020

EMERALD
BD Emerald Misc Color 2020

Roylac
BD Roylac 2021

Twentysix years of hundred-sixtysix Typedifferent fonts

1995–2021

www.typedifferent.com

The sunny side of typography is experimenting with the visual language.

Readability is the underwear – Originality is a dress code.

Titles and logotypes with original typefaces stimulate readers curiosity. Little extra effort to decipher letters will pay off in better recognizability.

Typefaces have different stylistic dialects. It is good to speak the same language as the readers.

Typographic rules are here to break. Letters gain character by interfering with their readability.

New shapes for typefaces can be found in unreadable things. Inspiration for new alphabets is all around.

If a font looks outdated at the moment – The font is probably just some years ahead?

A perfect font suffers from personality.

Black and white are the colours of letters. Gray is the colour of text.

Last but not least: A font is never complete.

4M PRINTING DEVELOPING

EKI SNAPSHOTS 15

NEGATIVE WALLET

CAMERA OPERATING MANUAL

★ RENS XD TITAN

Rx/7 INSTRUCTIONS

BLITZ 13

N NIGONS

PHOTO GRAPHY

ASA 600

COLOR POCKET

pictures from your CAMERA

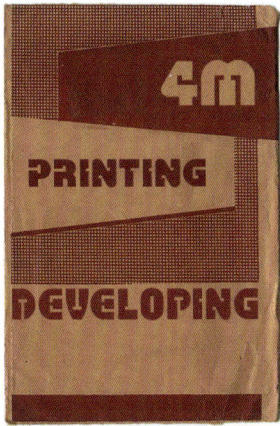

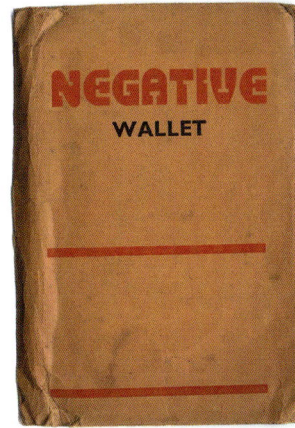

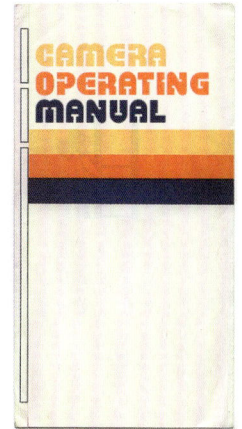

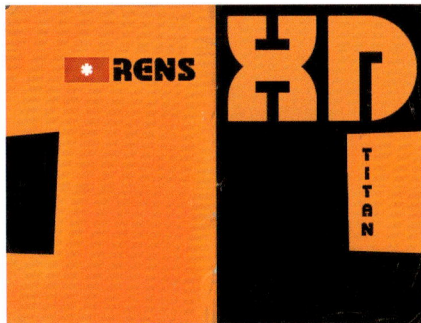

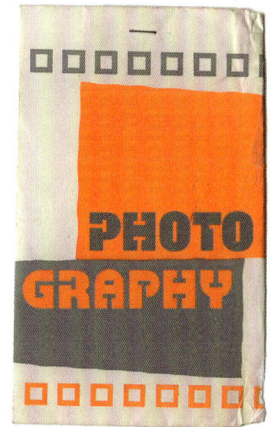

BD HitBit
Typedifferent font

2009
www.typedifferent.com

AB3CDDEEFFGHIJKLMMNOPPOR
RSTUUUVWXYYZZ1234567890

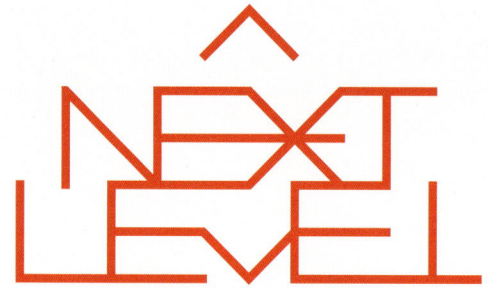

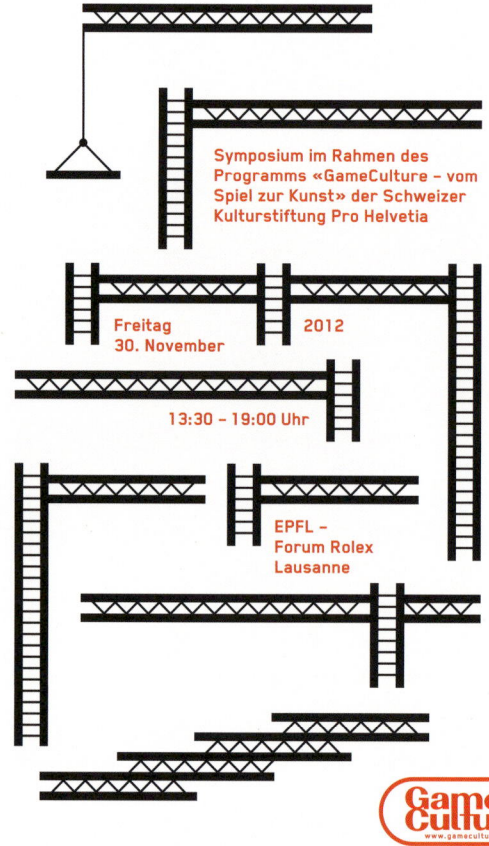

Top:
Spielplatz Schweiz
Programme booklet
cover for Deutsche
Gamestage, Berlin.
210 × 105 mm

Client:
Schweizer Kulturstiftung
Pro Helvetia

2012

Bottom Left:
Hans Dampf
Anniversary party
invitation flyer
74 × 105 mm

Client:
Hans Rufer

2013

Bottom Right:
140 Jahre Meer
Anniversary event deco-
rations for the furniture
company "Meer AG".
895 × 1280 mm

Client:
Panache
Kommunikation

2015

Right:
**Game Culture –
Next Level**
Programme booklet cover
for a symposium.
105 × 210 mm

Client:
Schweizer Kulturstiftung
Pro Helvetia

2012

Symposium im Rahmen des
Programms «GameCulture – vom
Spiel zur Kunst» der Schweizer
Kulturstiftung Pro Helvetia

Freitag   2012
30. November

13:30 – 19:00 Uhr

EPFL –
Forum Rolex
Lausanne

HANS *DAMPFT*
AB!
28. DEZEMBER
21:00 H
DAMPFZENTRALE
BERN

BD

140 Jahre Meer
Anniversary event
poster for the
furniture company
"Meer AG", Bern.
895 × 1280 mm

Client:
Panache
Kommunikation

2015

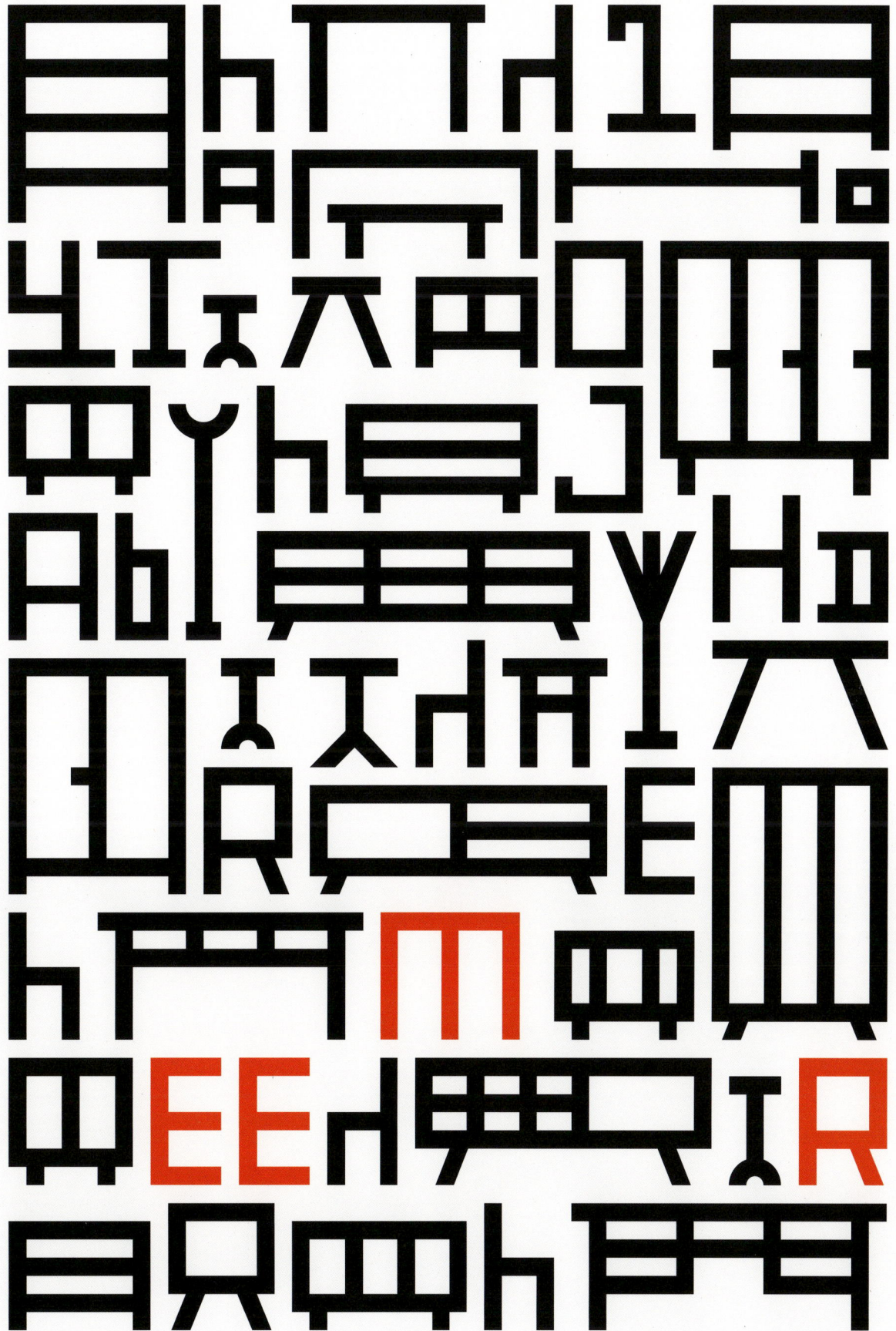

Leben in der Bärau
Illustration for an exhibition
wall telling the story of the
inhabitants of the poorhouse
and the emerging economy in
the village of Bärau, Emmental.

Internship collaboration
with Nathan Tomaschett

Client:
Stiftung Lebensart,
Ruedi Kunz & Jürg Spichiger
(Palma3)

2019

Cowshed Neocolor Box
Illustration for a give-away

Client:
Federal Department
of Foreign Affairs FDFA,
Presence Switzerland

2019

VISION Festival
Posters and flyers
297 × 420 mm
420 × 594 mm
594 × 841 mm

Client:
DekaDance

2010

THE NEXT CHAPTER
OPEN-AIR FESTIVAL
SWITZERLAND

deka dance

PRESENTS

VISION

SA 28 & SO 29

8

28./29. August

先見

2010

MORE INFOS SOON!

dekadance.ch

WWW

vision-festival.com

SVEN VÄTH

RICHIE HAWTIN

RICARDO VILLALOBOS

& MANY MORE

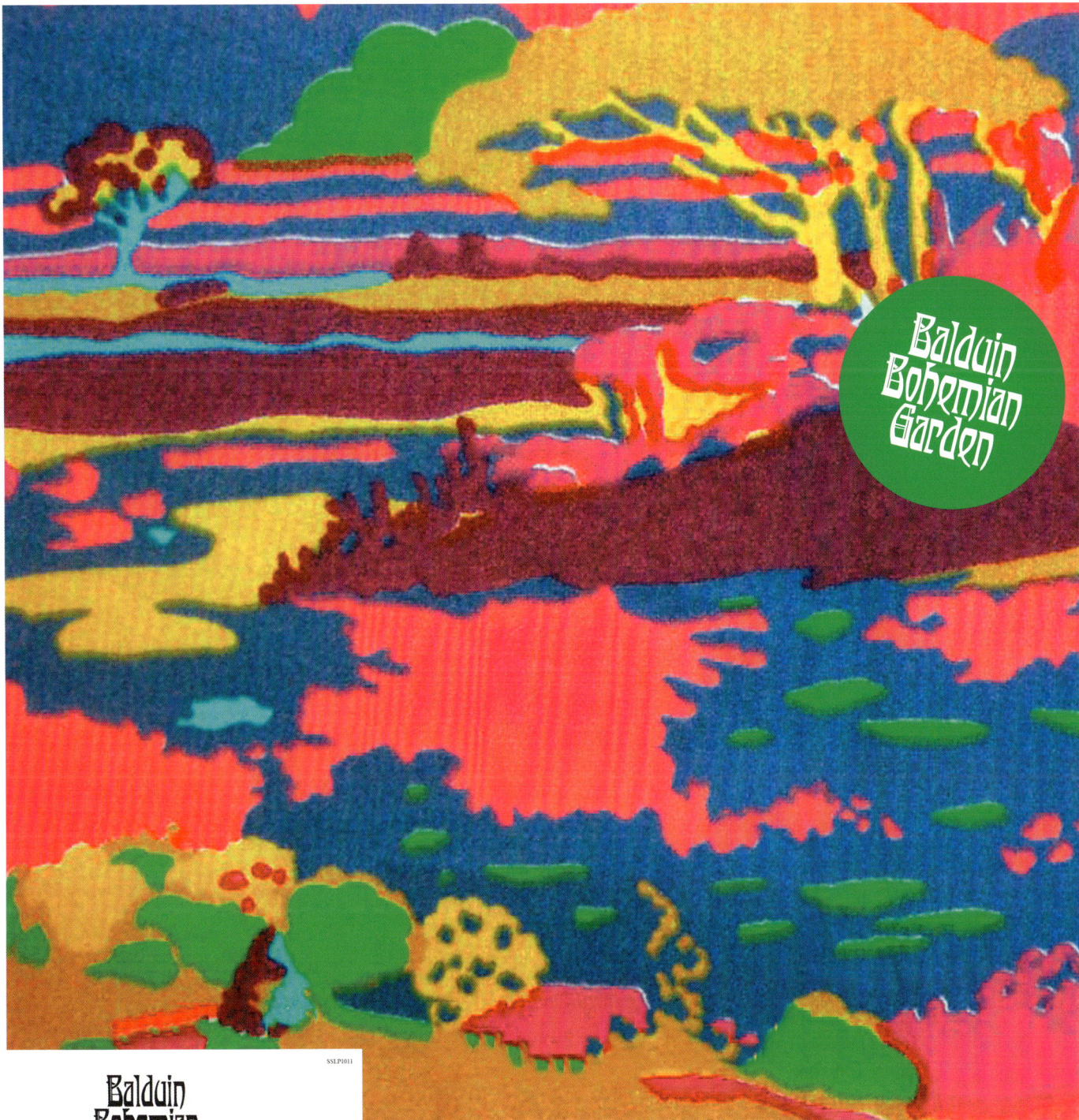

Side One
1 Bohemian Garden
2 Leave To Seek The Light
3 Cap Fréhel
4 I Am Here And You Are There
5 St. John's Shop
6 Your Own

Side Two
1 Libelle
2 Madrigal
3 A Song For The Moon
4 Teeny Weeny Queen
5 Mr. Bat
6 Rondo Vampyros

All songs written & recorded by Balduin at Creative Cookery Studio Bern, except «Madrigal» written by P. Morris, «St. John's Shop» written by W. Proctor. Textile paint by Unknown. Sleeve designed at Büro Destruct by Lopetz & Balduin.

STEREO

Balduin – Bohemian Garden
LP sleeve artwork

Published by Sun Stone
Records, Chester, UK

Client:
Sun Stone Records,
Balduin

2017

www.balduin.org

BD:247

WALKING

Walking Heads Organisation
Rebellion Street Art Initiative
WHO

Signs and symbols may not heal the world but they encourage action.
Given that we use them for the right and positive thing.

EADS ORG.

WHO

Submarie 8
Theater poster
and postcard
895×1280 mm
594×420 mm
148×210 mm

Client:
Theater Club 111

2020

BD Roylac
Typedifferent font

2020
www.typedifferent.com

Dedicated to Monsieur
Roy La Combe

Inspired by lowercase letters
designed by Jacques Loison in 1972

Lee Schornoz – London Tapes
CD sleeve artwork

Client:
Lee Schornoz

2020

LEE SCHORNOZ
LONDON TAPES

1. WEATHER FORECAST
2. BOTUSANA TWIST
3. MEXICO CALLS
4. BEAT MACHINE
5. BIRD RELOAD
6. AAKULUPE
7. GROOVE MY ASS
8. TO CUT A REAL LIFE STORY SHORT
9. SUNDAY JAM
10. FUCK OF THE END OF THE WORLD
11. WORLDMUSIC
12. CROATIAN'S BEAUTY'S GONE

PRO STATA RECORDS
WARSZAWA POLSKA

PSR016

LEE
SCHORNOZ
LONDON
TAPES

BD:253

Homeoffice

1st Floor:
71 sm
9 Seats
10 Tables
6 Monitors
6.5 m Books

Heinz "H1" Reber
Christoph Jenni
Jérôme Blum
Michael Zumstein

2nd Floor:
30.2 sm
5 Seats
4 Tables
2 Monitors
2.5 m Books

Marc "MB" Brunner

2nd Floor:
22.2 sm
4 Seats
2 Tables
2 Monitors
10.6 m Books

Lorenz "Lopetz"
Gianfreda

BD:254

büro destruct ビュロ デストラクト

future

Bureau de Struct

l'avenir du futur

BD:255

Thanks to all backers of Büro Destruct 4, who helped in making this publication possible.

Following people backed the Kickstarter campaign with the name-dropping package.
Thank you very much! Büro Destruct & Slanted Publishers

Adrian Susin • Aleksi Kinnunen • Alex Meireles Machado • Alexander Stern • Ana • André M. Pennycooke • Anna Meyer • Bryan Dunn • Cécile • Chris Corrado • Christoph Schreiber • Christophe • Cimbri • Daniel Nisttahuz • Dario Carta – #cartadesign • David OReilly • DJ Donovan™ • Drawcula • Esther Jenni • Ferenz Poor • Götz Ulmer • Gregory Ruben Salgado • HA-N5 VV-UR-5T • iD visuelle Kommunikation GmbH • Isaiah Whisner • Jason Armstrong • Jean-David Gadina • John Sherman Hoyt • Kat Ford • Lara Assouad • Lee Connett • Lee H. Mee • Manoske • Matteo Emme • Metanet Software Inc. • Nicholas Blaske • No Name • Not Another Graphic Designer • Oliver Amonn • Oliver Sung • Pablo Franco • Paolo Pavan • Pascal Staub • Paul Maeda • Rachel Roth • Rispler&Rispler Designer • schwindl • Sibyl Matter • Soren SMI Mikkelsen • SpirulineBienne • Stefano Cendron • Svet Simov / Fontfabric • Terence Bergagna • Thomas • Tobias Lauer • Tom Smoker • Trenton Wynter Brown • Tyson Steele • Xavier Alejandro • Yuki sabakichi Kinoshita

Thanks to our families, friends and clients:

Adrian Junker • Adrian Maissen • Adrien Laubscher • Alfred Marti • Anaïs Elisa Kohler • André Bex & Pichi Nahuel • Andrea Schulz • Ane Hebeisen • Annette Junker • Ardo Ardhana • Ariane Wavre • Ata Bozaci • Barbara Luethi Cappiello • Barbara Ryser • Beatrix Jutzler • Boris Hoppek & Dunja Jankovic • Boris Lehmann • Brigitte Pfister • Céline "C-Line" Quadri • Christian Calame • Christian Gusset • Christian Sommerhalder • Christian Wüthrich • Christoph Balmer • Christoph Balsiger • Christoph Berger & Ena Bartlome Berger • Christoph Jenni • Christoph Koller • Christoph Streubel • Claudia Gerdes • Claudia Kaufmann • Claudio "Balduin" & Junko Gianfreda • Connie Etter • Corso Bertozzi • Dani Rolli • Daniel Schueler • Daniel Wihler • Dimitri Sutter • Dorothea Stotzer • Elle Lanz • Esther Jenni Family Brunner • Family Gianfreda • Family Leihsa-Hebbeln • Family Reber • Family Uldry • Family Widmer • Family Wymann • Ferenz Poor • Francis Foss Pauchard • Franz Ermel • Franziska Jenkins • Gabriela Graber • German Heiniger • Grazia Pergoletti • Gregory Chapuisat • Guy Lafranchi • Haki Cakmak & Marc Kölla • Heidy-Jo Wenger • Hiromi Hosoya • Housi Rufener • Isabelle Bentz • Jacqueline Wehrle • Jan Galega Brönnimann • Jan Tümer • Jared Muralt • Jérôme Blum • Jim Avignon • Johannes Eggimann • Julia Kahl • Junko Hanzawa • Jürg & Mirco Leano Brunner • Jürg Junker • Jürg Spichiger • Karin Brülisauer • Kaspar Lüthi • Kathy Flück • Kazue Schmitt • Kazumi Kawakatsu • Kentaro "Ani" Fujimoto • Kevin Mueller • Lars Harmsen • Lea Niederhäuser • Leila Benaissa • Lionel Friedli • Louis Schornoz • Lucy Verlanova • Lukas Liederer • Luzia Häfliger • Maddie Caleff • Madeleine Corbat • Marcel Birrer • Marco Repetto • Mariana Da Cruz • Marie-Anne Reber • Marie-Françoise Keller • Mario Batkovic • Markus Reichenbach • Markus Schäfer • Martin Hägler • Martin Schneider • Mary Cartier • Matu Hügli • Maya Burri-Hueberli • Mayumi & Nara Tsuji Gianfreda • Meret Matter • Merja Rinderli • Mich Gerber • Mich Meienberg • Michael "Bataais" Gianfreda • Michael Sasdi • Michael Zumstein • Mickey Eskimo • Mie Owashi • Mirjam & Gil Zufferey • Monic Gyr • Monika Lehmann • Monique Sutter • Moritz Adler • Nadia Schweizer • Nadja Portmann • Nicolette Kretz • Nina Kern • Nina Meyer • Ondrej Kolacek • Pamela Jegerlehner • Patrick Bühler • Patrizia Tribolet • Pedä Siegrist • Pete Stiefel • Peter Fankhauser • Peter Treu • Philipp Pongracz • Philipp Thöni • Pia Affolter • Priska Krebs • Raphael Urweider • Regula Staub • Renate Wünsch • Remo Stoller • Robert Riesen • Rodja Galli • Roger Moser • Roland Baumberger • Roman Schären • Ruedi Kunz • Ryuko Kazumoto • Sabine Eva Wittwer • Sabine Kreienbühl • Sam Geiser • Samora "Oibel One" Bazarrabusa • Sarah Louise Junker • Severin Aegerter • Sibyl Matter • Sibylle Heiniger • Silvio Brügger • Simon Fehlmann • Sonja Kleinlogel • Sonja Kräuliger • Stefan Riesen • Stefan Wolf • Stéphanie Peter • Steve Zeidler • Susanne Tschan • Syl Hillier • Sylvain Gardel • Thomas Brändle • Thomas Brönnimann • Thomas Gloor • Thomas Niederhäuser • Thomas Weibel • Till Könneker • Tina Blaser • Todd Levin • Tonino de Rosa • Urs Althaus • Urs Zaugg • Ursula Brunner • Ursula Merki • Vera Gärttling • Viktor Uhlmann • Vincent Membrez • Wendelin, Monika, Noelia & Moritz Reber • Werner Tschan • Willi Brunner • Wim Louis Pepe Junker • Yukiko Yano • Zera Huber

And our interns over all the years:

Andrea Schulz • Angela Pestalozzi • Casper Herselman • Christoph Engelhard • Dana Purcz • Esther Nilsen • Florian Bendele • Gregory Temple Tate • Henrik Gytz Thorsager • Jacqueline Wehrle • Katrin Jachmann • Ly Thanh Le • Malaïka Schürch • Martin Lötscher • Max Henschel • Michael Fuchs • Nadine Schemmann • Natalie Birkle • Nathan Tomaschett • Nicole Nicolaus • Nina Yepuni Kern • Noëmi Gschwend-Droux • Peter Korsman • Remo Stoller • Rotjana Linz • Sabine Schäfer • Sarah Grandjean • Sebastian Hirn • Stefanie Läderach • Syl Hillier • Thomas Kurppa • Tuloan Huynh • Yukiko Yano